101
WAYS TO BOOST
YOUR BUSINESS

ALSO BY ANDREW GRIFFITHS

101 Ways to Market Your Business
101 Ways to Satisfy Your Customers
101 Ways to Advertise Your Business
Secrets to Building a Winning Business

COMING SOON

101 Ways to Balance Your Business and Your Life
101 Ways to Build a Network Marketing Business

101
WAYS TO BOOST YOUR BUSINESS

ANDREW GRIFFITHS

ALLEN&UNWIN

First published in 2002 under the title *101 Survival Tips For Your Business*
This revised edition published in 2006

Allen & Unwin
83 Alexander Street
Crows Nest NSW 2065
Australia
Phone: (61 2) 8425 0100
Fax: (61 2) 9906 2218
Email: info@allenandunwin.com
Web: www.allenandunwin.com

National Library of Australia
Cataloguing-in-Publication entry:

Griffiths, Andrew, 1966– .
   101 ways to boost your business.
   ISBN 978 1 74175 006 5.

   ISBN 1 74175 006 7.

   1. Success in business – Handbooks, manuals. 2. Industrial
   management – Handbooks, manuals, etc. I. Title.

658.155

Set in 12/14 pt Adobe Garamond by Midland Typesetters, Australia
Printed in Australia by McPherson's Printing Group

10 9 8 7 6 5 4 3 2 1

Contents

Acknowledgments

The information contained in this book is based on my observations of many successful businesses. I would like to express my thanks to those individuals who have given me their thoughts, views and suggestions.

I would also like to thank the team at Allen & Unwin who have inspired me to keep writing. You are a dynamic team and quite simply some of the most professional and supportive people I have ever worked with. I consider myself very lucky to be writing for such an impressive publishing company.

As with every project that I do, I have had enormous support from my family and friends. Their words of encouragement mean everything to me.

Finally, a special thank you to all the readers who have purchased my books. I am constantly surprised by the number of letters, faxes and emails that I receive from readers around the world. To those people who take the time to pass on words of appreciation, thank you very much. Your kind words mean a lot.

Introduction

In the daily course of my work as a marketing consultant I spend a lot of time talking to successful business people. Without exception, these individuals have a wealth of knowledge and experience that they apply to their businesses and which makes them successful. We often laugh about how much easier things would have been if we could have applied what we know now to our early business ventures, but most of us have had to learn the hard way, which has often cost us a lot of money and heartache.

Over almost 20 years in business I have heard the same comments time and time again. In recent years I have realised that all businesses seem to experience the same basic problems and that most of these problems could have been avoided with the help of some simple, practical advice. Hence, I have written this book.

My first book, *101 Ways to Market Your Business*, was written to help anyone who owns or operates a business to increase profitability by introducing some very simple marketing ideas. These ideas were developed around three key principles: that people trying to promote a business often lack the time to devote to marketing, lack the money to spend on marketing, and lack basic marketing knowledge. The book was written in very simple, jargon-free language, and the ideas suggested produce very tangible results.

101 Ways to Boost Your Business follows the same principles. It is written in short blocks that make it easy to find and quickly read information that is practical, relevant and realistic.

It is not filled with hype, or with ideas that sound great but prove impossible to implement.

By reading this book you will save yourself a lot of stress and money. Most people in business have to learn what to do the hard way. These mistakes may send them broke and cause myriad associated health and family problems.

But this book is all about boosting your business. Today there is no point simply surviving. If you were happy to do that you would stay working for someone else. In reality, this book will show you how to make your business so much better than your competitors in every way. It will boost what you do and you will reap the rewards. Now that is what every business owner wants to hear.

Who is this book written for?

101 Ways to Boost Your Business is written for the person who wants to make a difference. If you think you know everything there is to know about business, you probably wouldn't be reading this book. If you are flicking through the pages because you are keen to try and find ways to be better at what you do and to increase your chances of building a booming business, then you are looking in the right place.

101 Ways to Boost Your Business is written for anyone who has a key role within a business. It is for managers, owners and operators, prospective business buyers, students studying business, marketing managers, operations managers and professional advisers. It crosses all boundaries and provides information about issues that any person involved in business for any length of time will encounter.

It is written in a way that makes it universally applicable. The information contained in this book is as relevant to a bakery owner in Belgium as it is to a bookshop owner in Brisbane. The principles and tips discussed here are important to *all* businesses, regardless of their type or geographical location.

The real value of *101 Ways to Boost Your Business*

As mentioned earlier, *101 Ways to Boost Your Business* is a book based entirely upon experience. Many of the experiences are mine, a large number are those of people I have met and dealt with over the years and some are a combination of both.

Many people take a lifetime in business to become aware of these booster tips. I wish that I had had access to a book such as this when I started my first business almost 20 years ago. Hopefully, you will read *101 Ways to Boost Your Business* and avoid making the mistakes that I, and many other business operators, have made. This book provides you with the opportunity to learn from the experiences of many successful business operators and entrepreneurs, and to dramatically boost your own chances of business survival and success.

The advice and suggestions included in this book have been given freely by friends and business associates who, while successful now, had to learn their lessons the hard way. For me, a truly successful person is one who is willing to share the secrets of their success with others, giving freely of their time and advice and expecting nothing in return.

How to get the most out of this book

101 Ways to Boost Your Business has been written in such a way that it can be opened at any page and the advice used immediately. There are a total of 121 booster tips included, covering the areas that most commonly cause businesses to falter. Some of the tips may not be relevant to you at this moment in time, but if you pick up the book again in six months' time, the tips that you glossed over on your first reading may now be relevant. For this reason, I recommend that you keep *101 Ways to Boost Your Business* handy. Don't put it away at the top of your bookcase: keep it in your briefcase, or in a drawer in your desk, or leave it by the telephone or on your bedside table. Consider it as a constant source of inspiration and advice that is available to you 24 hours a day.

Some people avoid reading the preliminary sections of books, preferring to get right into it. If that describes you, no problem; just start flicking through the pages and see which booster tips spark your interest. If you prefer to start at the beginning and read every page, then make yourself a cup of coffee, find a comfortable chair, and start reading.

This is a practical book that needs to be referred to often. Cut out or photocopy the blank forms in the appendix to the book and fill them in, highlight sections of the text that you find relevant to your own situation, and write notes in the spaces provided at the end of each section.

One last point before you get started

Throughout this book you are going to read the word 'boost' a lot—pretty much on every page. To boost means to lift; to raise; to generally improve. Without a doubt that is the message behind this book. Every time you see the word 'boost', let it sink in and remember that boost equates to making your business better and that equates to success, profitability and an overwhelming sense of satisfaction. Love that word.

1 | The future of small business

Small businesses form the backbone of many economies. As populations grow worldwide, so do the number of small businesses starting up. Millions of people around the world continue to opt for running their own business instead of working for larger organisations. As a result, there is an incredible knowledge and skill base tied up in running these small businesses. There is an enormous amount of expertise and specialist knowledge that thrives in this economic sector, the value of which is often underestimated.

From my experience, small businesses generally offer far better levels of service than do their larger counterparts. This is due, in most instances, to the key personnel being involved at the front of the business. They deal with their customers face to face, and the business is small enough to ensure that communication is open and continual.

There is no doubt that there are many trials and tribulations when it comes to running your own business and, of course, there is the ever-present risk of financial failure. However, this doesn't seem to deter people from choosing this alternative career path, and for that I think they should be admired.

The problem facing most small businesses is the ever-increasing competition from other small businesses. This dilemma is here to stay; in fact, it will only increase. With the advent of the Internet and other new technologies, the competition that we all face now comes not only from the business up the road, but from businesses on the other side of the world.

Small businesses need to be smart. They need to be built on solid foundations and to be proactive. They need continually to strive to provide exceptional levels of customer service and value for money. Consumers are better informed and more discerning than ever before, and are well aware that they have a lot of choice when it comes to deciding on where they will spend their hard-earned money.

Business survival is about facing these ongoing challenges with a commitment to being the best at what you do. It is about treating consumers with the respect that they deserve, while standing out from the sea of other businesses that offer the same or similar services.

It's all about attitude

From my experience, there are two very distinct types of businesses and business operators.

There are those people who are really unhappy doing what they do. Everyone else is to blame for the problems they experience. The customers are an inconvenience, and are always causing problems. Advertising is just a waste of time and money. The accountants are no good, the staff are nothing but trouble, and the future always looks glum. These businesses struggle to survive.

The other type of business that I have observed is run by positive and enthusiastic people. They take what they do seriously, they believe in offering excellent customer service and value for money, and they are continually looking for ways to make their business better. They don't act like victims. If they face a setback, as we all do from time to time, they pick themselves up, dust themselves off and get on with it. They dwell on the positive, rather than the negative, aspects of the situation. These businesses have a far better chance of surviving and flourishing than the first type, due, I believe, to the attitude of the business operator. From my experience, there are more of the negative types of businesses than there are the positive ones. So, the first step to boosting your business is to ensure that you have the right attitude about running your business.

If you already own or operate a business . . .

People who have been running their own or someone else's business for a long time are often set in their ways. They may have formed bad business habits and may regard 'change' as a dirty word. I doubt that this describes you, because if it did, it's unlikely that you would have purchased this book.

The greatest personality trait that any business person can have is an open mind. We live in an age where there is an over-abundance of information, a lot of it conflicting. The fact is that the amount of information available is only going to increase, so we need to be able to use this wealth of information for our own benefit.

Successful business people have two striking characteristics: a very clear objective combined with an air of detachment about their business. I have run a number of businesses that were unprofitable because, while I had the clear objective, I didn't have the air of detachment. The clear objective gives you the passion and the enthusiasm to keep going, but the detachment stops the business from taking over your life. It enables you to be somewhat clinical about what you are doing: if it's not working, let it go.

This book will provide you with direction and simple step-by-step blocks of information that may direct your passion and enthusiasm; however, learning to be detached is a much harder skill to master. A business is just a business. There is life before, during and after. If you are not enjoying, or worse still you hate, what you are doing, maybe it's time to cut your losses and make a break. Detachment lets you do this.

If I had learned to let go at an earlier age, I would have saved myself a lot of grief. Now I find it easy. If it's not working and I know that I have given it 100 per cent, I will simply cut my losses and move on. There will be other business opportunities that will come my way and, most importantly, I will have learned a few new lessons.

The topics covered in this book

Based on my own experiences and those of the people I have spoken to regarding their own business tips, 11 key categories were developed for *101 Ways to Boost Your Business*. They cover all of the areas that virtually any business will need to deal with at some stage in the history of their organisation.

While some of the tips deal with very specific issues, such as ensuring that you have enough money to run your business, there are also more general tips on how to overcome the personal pressures and strains of running your own business. Each type of booster tip is equally important. There are many ways to determine whether or not a business is successful, and a profit and loss statement is only one way.

The topics covered include:

- getting advice booster tips;
- financial booster tips;
- business relationship booster tips;
- staff booster tips;
- customer service booster tips;
- advertising and marketing booster tips;
- Internet booster tips;
- insurance booster tips;
- legal booster tips;

- personal booster tips; and
- planning for the future booster tips.

The bonus section includes a further 20 booster tips that incorporate all of the above topics.

About the blank forms

The blank forms in the appendix at the back of *101 Ways to Boost Your Business* have been included to illustrate a number of booster tips. They can be photocopied and reused as necessary. Most are checklists that can be filed in the relevant places and used as needed.

I have also included an outline of the information you need to develop your own simple marketing plan. This may sound like a complicated project, but in reality it is easy. Marketing plans evolve and need to be updated on a regular basis, but there is no doubt that having a simple marketing plan will be of significant benefit to your business.

The blank forms include:

- a credit request form (for your customers);
- a goals and objectives form;
- a professional services checklist;
- a checklist for employing staff;
- a job description form (position description);
- a step-by-step marketing plan;
- an insurance summary page;
- a stress checklist;
- a de-stress checklist; and
- an outline for developing an Internet plan.

There is also space to write notes at the end of each section on any action you need to take regarding specific booster tips.

2 | Getting advice booster tips

We all need help and advice at some stage in our business career. Knowing when, and where, to get advice are the two main issues. Both issues are outlined in this section, and a number of ideas are suggested that could prove to be not only booster tips but also very financially rewarding.

The ideas we'll talk about in this section are:

#1   What type of help is available?
#2   Know when to look for help
#3   Embrace technology and save money
#4   You might be eligible for a grant

1 What type of help is available?

There are so many organisations available to assist business operators that it's sometimes hard to know where to start looking. There are various government-run organisations, as well as many private enterprises, that offer thousands of products and services that could be of benefit to you.

If you are planning on starting a business, do your homework now. Find out about these organisations and exactly what services they provide. Government-run organisations generally have the distinct advantage of offering their products and services for free or at fairly reasonable rates. Private enterprises tend to charge a little more, but from my experience they generally provide faster and more detailed services. This, of course, varies from area to area, and I have worked with many government-run organisations that are excellent. If you are not sure who to use, talk to other business people.

If you already run your own business, it's often very beneficial to visit your local business advisory board to find out exactly what services they offer. You may find that help is available for exactly the kind of problems you are experiencing. One thing is certain: whatever the problem you have, other businesses have had similar problems and somewhere there will be help available.

I also like to utilise a network of business associates. If I am experiencing a specific problem, I make a few calls to my circle and ask for their advice; they do likewise. We all talk to each other regularly, and we honour confidentiality when an associate tells us about a problem that they are experiencing. This mutual assistance works very well and can save you an enormous amount of time and money.

Developing your own similar network can provide your business with a free pool of experience that is on tap for you to use whenever you need it. I think it is important to ensure that there is an equal amount of information exchanged, otherwise your associates may start to groan every time you call. If someone gives me some great information that will save me money or time, I like to send them a small gift and a note expressing my thanks.

There are also excellent books available that include lists of organisations and what services they provide. Talk to your local bookstore and they can generally point you in the right direction. I use a reference book for writers that lists thousands of companies and government organisations that offer various products and services to writers.

Individual industries normally have their own associations that are great sources of information. By being a member, you will have access to information that would normally be hard to find. The best thing about these organisations is that they already know and understand your business, and the odds are that your problems are shared by other businesses in the same industry.

Of course, the Internet provides access to vast quantities of information, and I recommend that you spend some time searching for help online.

Finding out what type of help is available takes only time. Increase your chances of boosting your business by being well informed about who to turn to for help when you need it.

2 Know when to look for help

One of the most common characteristics of successful business people is that they are not afraid to ask questions or to seek help when they need it. We all need help in some form or another at some time.

If you are having financial problems, talk to your accountant. If you are having legal problems, talk to your lawyer. The longer you wait, the worse the problem will be. I have often spent many hours worrying about a specific problem when it could have been solved with a simple phone call. We might worry that our accountant or lawyer will think we are stupid if we ask a dumb question. Who cares? What is important is that the problem gets solved quickly and with the minimum of fuss.

We have a client who specialises in handling companies' affairs when they go broke. They often comment that if they had been called in earlier, nine times out of ten they could have helped the business to recover and prevented an enormous amount of stress and worry. Unfortunately, many people wait until the bank is ready to foreclose or the landlord has issued the eviction notice before looking for help.

Just like an illness, most business problems can be cured if they are detected early and the proper treatment is implemented. If you want to boost your business, don't wait until it is too late for anyone to help you.

3 Embrace technology and save money

I am often surprised by the number of business operators who don't utilise technology. Technology, by definition, is an advancement or development that enables a task to be done better. If the task can be done better, it can generally be done quicker and hence more economically.

Some people are scared of technology generally, which is understandable when you think about how fast it changes. There are others who fear the cost of technology, and those who simply don't feel they have the time to find out about new technologies.

I encounter all of these types of business operators every day and, without exception, I can see ways in which they could not only *save* money, but also *make* more money in terms of more sales, simply by utilising technology.

One example that comes to mind in our business is the invention of the digital camera. If a client needs a photograph quickly, we can send someone over with a digital camera who takes the photo, comes back to the office, downloads it and emails it to the customer (sometimes after touching it up a little to make it clearer and sharper). The whole process may take ten minutes. In the past we had to obtain the film, take the photograph, drop the film at the film processor's and wait for it to be developed, scan the picture and then send it to the client. Obviously, the new method is much faster and more economical for the client.

Boosting your business is all about working smarter than your opposition. Spending money on technology is not only tax deductible, it's also logical. What is the point of using an old printer that jams every time you try to print a document? You get frustrated and angry because you don't want to spend the money on a new one, yet you will spend hours every day removing jammed paper from your old printer. Don't forget that your time is valuable and is better spent focusing on running your business at its peak.

In today's business environment there are virtually no industries that are exempt from enjoying new technology. The key is to find out about it, and there is no shortage of places to find information on new products and services that may help your business to run better.

4 You might be eligible for a grant

Many governments around the world offer incentives for people to run small businesses. These governments realise that small businesses play a major role in their economy (as they have done for thousands of years) by distributing products and services to the general public.

They are also aware that small businesses provide jobs for millions of people, which in turn provides money to spend on goods and services, which keeps the economy turning. This means that by having lots of healthy small businesses operating, more people will be able to find work. If jobs are created, governments get re-elected and the cycle continues.

Because of this motivation, you may find that your business is eligible for some kind of grant or special funding. Often government incentives relate to employing people, an expense that most businesses try to keep as low as possible.

Recently, we employed a young receptionist who was part of a government training program. The conditions were that she work for our firm for one year, in return for which her wages were heavily subsidised and our business was given cash incentives throughout the year. We were required to assist with training, and the employee was expected to learn valuable business skills that she could use to further her career. We enjoyed lower wage costs and a motivated trainee who was keen to learn.

There are many such schemes in place. Some are easy to find out about, while others need researching. My advice is to start looking for information on the Internet and then spread your search further afield from there. Talking to other business operators is an excellent way to find out about government schemes, and a visit to your local small business advisory centre should also provide you with some leads.

If you still hit dead ends, contact your local politician and ask them about any incentives in place to help your business. If there aren't any, ask them why not. You may be entitled to receive some form of funding to help your business grow, and not even be aware of it.

Notes

....
....
....
....
....
....
....
....
....
....
....
....
....
....
....
....

Booster Tips Action List

Things to do   **Completed**

1. ....
2. ....
3. ....
4. ....
5. ....
6. ....
7. ....
8. ....
9. ....
10. ....

3 | Financial booster tips

Running a successful business really boils down to one critical point: making money. The booster tips in this section are aimed at identifying the areas where most of us make mistakes that can end up costing us money. We look at the reality of how much money you need to start or run a business, realistic budgets (not fairytales), keeping records (the bane of my life!), the importance of having a good accountant and how to find one, the cost of expanding, and knowing how much you should be charging for your goods and services.

The section also discusses the pitfalls of expansion, how to know when you are in financial trouble and, most importantly, what to do about it. This is an important section, because it's the area where most businesses perish.

The ideas we'll talk about in this section are:

#5 Don't be undercapitalised—have enough money from the start
#6 Budgets and planning—welcome to reality (plan for the worst, not the best)
#7 Financing—it pays to shop around
#8 Keep your personal and business records separate
#9 Find and use a good accountant
#10 What's the difference between an accountant and a financial planner?

#11 What to do if you get into financial trouble
#12 The real cost of expanding—can you afford it?
#13 Beware of giving credit
#14 Chasing bad debts—is it worth it?
#15 Keep good records from the start
#16 Keeping costs down without losing customers
#17 How to know what to charge
#18 Don't invest your superannuation in a business venture
#19 Beware the third-year boom and fourth-year bust

5 Don't be undercapitalised—have enough money from the start

I bought my first business for $22,500. The asking price was $25,000 and I negotiated the price down. The owner agreed to my offer, and I went to the bank and borrowed the money. The cheque was handed over and suddenly I was running my own dive shop. I have to say, I felt pretty pleased with myself!

Unfortunately, I started making mistakes the minute I handed over the cheque. I borrowed just enough money to buy the business and not one cent more. I was immediately inundated with bills as a result of the sale. They included accountant's fees, state taxes, legal fees, and so on, totalling about $5000, which, of course, I didn't have. Also, I had purchased the dive shop at the beginning of winter—the quietest time of year for this kind of business. Some of the equipment was old and needed to be replaced, and the level of stock was very low. All in all, I had got off to a pretty bad start. In many ways the business never really recovered, because I was always seriously short of money.

If I could turn back the clock and use the experience I now have, how would I have approached this same situation? First, I would have negotiated much harder on the sale price. The previous owner wasn't making any money and, in hindsight, I probably could have bought the business for next to nothing. Second, I would have paid a mechanic or an engineer to check all of the equipment to determine whether it was in good condition and what would need to be replaced.

Finally, I would have worked out how much it was going to cost me to operate the business for a full year, taking into consideration all the expenses, including my wages. Once this figure was determined, I would have added it to the negotiated cost of the business. To this I would have added the cost of replacing any equipment that wasn't in good enough condition to last 12 months. Once a total figure had been determined, I would have added a 20 per cent contingency and the new total is how much money I would have tried to borrow from the bank. Obviously, I would be asking for a lot more money, but if I couldn't get the total amount I would have to think long and hard about buying the business in the first place.

Many people get caught up in the emotion of the moment when it comes to buying or starting a business. Their excitement about the new venture often overshadows their normally strong sense of reason. There is a lot to be said for having time to cool off and really consider the decision.

There are two types of businesses in the world: those that have experienced a lack of money, and those that will experience a lack of money. Nine times out of ten, a lack of money can be traced back to not having enough money from day one. I was in a position with my first business where I had to start making a profit from day one. Not just turning money over, but making a profit. This is very hard to do. When starting or buying a business, there are so many potential pitfalls that can affect income that there really are no certainties.

If you are starting a business, you will need to be sure that there are people who are prepared to buy your products. It will take you a while to establish your own customers and to build the business up to a level where you are covering costs. While you are building the business, you will still need to pay for all of your fixed expenses and this goes back to the amount of money you have available when starting your business (your start-up capital).

If you are buying someone else's business, you are buying a cash flow and existing customers (goodwill). Unfortunately, there is no guarantee that the customers will continue to use the business when you take it over. You need to allow for the fact that you may lose a certain proportion of these customers. I have seen this happen many times where a business is sold and the customers leave in droves. Often the new owner goes broke in a relatively short amount of time. This normally indicates that they didn't allow for the possible exodus of customers and didn't have sufficient capital behind them to cover these losses until they built up their own customers.

Owning and operating your own business can be incredibly rewarding. It's certainly a lot more enjoyable if you can reduce your stress levels by having good financial planning and a realistic approach to how much money it will take to get you to where you want to be. Ensuring that you have enough money to start or buy your business is essential.

6 Budgets and planning—welcome to reality (plan for the worst, not the best)

In Booster Tip #5 we talked about the problem of not having enough money when you start your business. This booster tip looks at setting budgets that are realistic and honest. In business we all need to set budgets. We need to know exactly how much it will cost to run our business and thus how much money we will need to cover those costs.

A common mistake in business is poor planning and unrealistic expectations in terms of income and expenses. From my experience, the three most common errors are:

- underestimating costs (expenses);
- overestimating how much money will come in (income); and
- failing to recognise that money will be slower coming in than expected.

Obviously, the end result of these errors is a serious lack of cash (or a cash flow problem).

This booster tip aims to encourage you to take a realistic approach to budgeting. Don't plan for the best possible scenario, plan for the worst. If everything turns out better than expected, you will end up with more money in the bank—an end result that is easy to live with.

When planning your expenses, take absolutely everything into consideration and then make an allowance for the out-of-the-ordinary or unexpected costs. A lot of expenses are easy to budget for because they come in month after month. Rent is a prime example—it's easy to budget for because it's roughly the same amount every month. Other expenses—such as bank fees, state and federal taxes, repairs to vehicles, breakdown of equipment, insurance, legal and accounting fees, and so on—are harder to plan for; however, allowance needs to be made for them.

As an example, let's assume that it costs you $10,000 per month in simple fixed costs to open your business doors. This includes all the expenses that you can budget for. (Even the small bills that are only a few dollars a week add up and have an effect on your bottom line.) Now you need to allow for unexpected costs. I budget for extra costs of 20 per cent per month on out-of-the-ordinary costs, and generally this more than covers those extra costs. Once again, if there are no out-of-the-ordinary costs I come out in front. Based on this principle, the costs to operate your business are now $12,000 per month. This tells you exactly how much money you need to make each month to cover your costs.

Overestimating the amount of income you can expect from your business is a very common mistake. We have to be optimistic to run a business, but there is a fine line between optimism and naivety. As far as I am concerned, income isn't guaranteed until the money is in the bank. I have been caught out many times by spending money that was definitely meant to come in, only to find that for some reason the project didn't go ahead.

We know how much money we need in order to operate, so we have an income target. When planning for income the same principle has to apply—be conservative, and underestimate rather than overestimate. If you are wrong, the worst that can happen is that you end up with more money in the bank than you anticipated. Only *you* can really set your budget for expected income. If your business has a history you can often plan fairly accurately based on previous years, but if you are starting a new business you sometimes have to make an educated guess. Be very careful of making assumptions that cannot be backed up.

I once worked with a company that started a new business in a shopping centre. They budgeted for 10 per cent of the people coming into the centre to visit their business. Obviously, this is a big assumption based on little apart from simple traffic flow. Other factors that influence this assumption relate to location, costs, competition, appeal of the business, staff, the fit-out of the shop, and so on. The business struggled for many years simply because the assumption that was made was wrong and overly positive. A common practice of good budget planners is to allow for both worst case and best case scenarios.

Like income, cash flow needs to be planned, especially if your business works on customers being given accounts. Often a business can be trading very well, with 'on the book profits' looking fantastic, but in reality there is never any money in the bank. Cash flow problems can destroy a business quicker than anything else. When planning for cash flow always be conservative, allow for delays and the odd bad debt, and have a back-up plan just in case cash flow becomes tight. Most cash flow problems stem from being undercapitalised (Booster Tip #1) from the start.

In closing, the most important point to be taken from this booster tip is that you need to be a realist when planning budgets. If you find this hard, seek advice from someone impartial, such as an accountant. Setting tight, conservative budgets is a trademark of successful businesses and it will certainly make running your business easier.

7 Financing—it pays to shop around

These days everyone wants to lend you money. If you have a reasonable credit rating, your letterbox will be filled with an abundance of amazing deals that will all put you further into debt. Financial institutions will treat you like you are the most important person in the world—until you sign on the dotted line. Then try being a week late with a car payment to find out what poor customer service is all about.

The truth about finance is that everyone will give it to you when you don't need it, but no one will give it to you when you do need it. That's the harsh reality, and in many ways it's understandable. Another reality is that if you don't own property of some kind, you will pay through the nose for any finance because you are considered a higher-risk borrower.

So, how does this affect you? First, try to avoid asking for credit when you are cash strapped or if you don't own property. A few years ago I went to the bank to ask for a $5000 overdraft. I had trading figures for several years which were reasonably good, but at the time I didn't own any property. The bank manager didn't even read my application. He simply said that I would be better off using one of my credit cards to get a cash advance if I needed extra money. The problem with this was that my credit cards were all attracting 17 per cent interest and I didn't want to pay that much, but I had no choice.

There have been many instances during my business career when times were tough and I needed extra cash to keep paying the bills. Desperate for money, I have had to resort to borrowing from a financial institution of some sort at a ridiculous rate, and ended up regretting it for years. For instance, I purchased a secondhand car about five years ago. The dealer arranged the finance very quickly, and before I knew it I was signing a contract. I borrowed $24,000 at 17.5 per cent interest and ended up paying back a fortune. Not once did I think to shop around, or to ask the lender for a better rate. At the time, banks and credit unions were offering car loans for about 9 per cent interest! Over five years this oversight cost me a lot of money, and I certainly won't be making the same mistake again.

Often when we approach a finance company, we do so with our hat in our hand almost begging them for the money. The irony of this is that they know it, and they encourage this kind of behaviour since they make a lot of money out of us. You should therefore shop around when looking for any kind of finance. Feel free to negotiate on interest rates. Now that I am older and a little wiser, I know that most financial institutions have some room to move; even if they can't budge on interest rates, they can waive fees and offer other incentives.

Remember, you are the customer and they stand to make a lot of money out of you.

8 Keep your personal and business records separate

A common mistake, especially among first-time business operators, is to fail to keep your personal records separate from your business records. There may be times when you pay a bill for the business with your own credit card or pay a personal bill, such as your electricity bill at home, with a company cheque. The problem with this is that it makes working out your tax return a lot more complicated, because you generally cannot claim personal expenses on your tax return. It also becomes a paperwork nightmare when you have to allocate where funds have come from or where they have gone to.

Of course, I have been guilty of doing this in the past. With my first business, I didn't even know that the two should be kept separate; I just assumed that all the receipts needed to be kept in the same shoebox. My first accountant was very patient. He had retired and I think that he felt sorry for me, so he very gently explained how the system worked and from that time on I have been reasonably good at it.

Another problem with mixing your business records with your personal records is that you can end up paying either not enough tax or too much tax. Both are potential problems and, generally, taxation departments are not all that understanding about poor bookkeeping practices. At the end of the day, you should know the difference; ignorance isn't an excuse.

I know a lot of business operators who are always putting their hand in their pockets to buy things for the business. It might only be a few dollars at a time but it all adds up. To overcome this, you need to have some petty cash—say, a few hundred dollars—that you use for these smaller purchases. The key with petty cash is to keep receipts to ensure that when it's all spent, the receipts equal the total amount. Then you write another cheque and start again.

Over the years, I have lost literally thousands of dollars in unclaimed expenses simply because I couldn't seem to get my head around the idea of petty cash.

It makes life a lot easier if you can start your business by keeping your records separate. If you have been operating for a few years and the areas are still overlapping, just start working towards separating the two as soon as possible. Your accountant should be helping you with this, but if you are still unsure invest a little time and do a bookkeeping course. If this still doesn't work, you need to employ someone to control your accounts who is ruthless and not intimidated by you being the boss. If you don't have the receipt, you don't get the money. No purchase order, no cheque. You get the message.

9 Find and use a good accountant

Having a good accountant is essential. Unfortunately, they are hard to find. The biggest complaint that I would make about accountants is that generally they aren't interested in my business unless it's making a lot of money. I agree that this is probably the most interesting and appealing time from the accountant's point of view, but I have been most in need of help and advice when things aren't going quite so well.

So, how do you find a good accountant? I took the following steps to find my current accountant, who is great. First, I picked up the Yellow Pages and picked out ten names that appealed to me for whatever reason (for example, I liked the colours in their advertisements). Then I rang ten business associates and asked them who they used and whether they would recommend them. Then I made appointments with the companies that matched. There were five firms in total that I was now considering.

During the appointments with each accountant, I interviewed them. I wanted them to tell me why I should use them, and I asked for the names of several of their clients so that I could verify that they were as good as they said they were. I wasn't rude or arrogant, but at the same time I wasn't intimidated by them. I wanted someone who would guide me and help me to build up my business. I was honest in telling them about the positive and negative features of my business and what I needed. It is important that you have these points clear in your own mind.

Two of the five firms refused to give me the names of people to verify their services, so they were out straight away. I rang each of the people whose names the three remaining firms had supplied, and I made my decision based on those people's comments. I must be honest and say that an important feature that I was looking for was an accountant with whom I could communicate easily. We needed to connect.

It's perfectly acceptable to discuss costs with your prospective accountant. In fact you would be crazy not to ask what their hourly rate is and for an approximation on annual costs. This way, there are no surprises for you or them. A common business mistake is people not asking how much something will cost until after the work is done. Then they complain about the expense. Good communication should eliminate this particular hazard.

Once you have decided upon an accountant, you need to start building a relationship. Don't be embarrassed about the state of your financial records or the fact that your business might not be making a lot of money. Accountants are like doctors. They won't tell anyone else, and they have generally seen it all before. Most importantly, you have to be completely honest with them. If your accountant submits your tax return based on the information that you have given them and it's not true, *you* get into trouble, not them. So be open and tell it the way it is.

If there are problems in the way you do things, your accountant should be working with you to help eliminate those problems. It may take a while, but as long as you are working together, virtually any problem can be overcome.

A good accountant is a powerful weapon in the arsenal required to survive in business. I believe that an accountant can only be as good as their client. Be open to their ideas, be honest and take their advice—after all, that's what you are paying them for.

10 What's the difference between an accountant and a financial planner?

This is a question that doesn't really have a clear answer. It's important to know that these services exist, because you need to know which one you may need at any time.

I use an accountant to make sure that all of my legal obligations are met. These include lodging periodical tax returns, documenting minutes to annual meetings and ensuring that all company fees are paid on time. My accountant is also there to advise me on ways to reduce my taxation where possible. He helps to identify legal ways to save tax, and makes recommendations for protecting my assets and limiting my liabilities. He also helps with my overall business strategy and planning for the long-term future of the business and myself.

I use a financial planner specifically to build my own wealth. My financial planner has arranged life insurance, superannuation, income protection policies and high-interest investments. His role is to take the money that I earn in my business and make it grow.

Confusion stems from the fact that many accountants are also financial planners. I believe that the two roles go very much hand in hand, but I like to have advice from two sources. If your business is anything like mine, in the early days there is no money. Paying the accountant is hard enough, and the idea of using a financial planner isn't even an option. As your business matures, you will find that you have some extra funds available and eventually there will be a time when you need to start thinking about what to do with this money.

Whichever way you want to go, and in a perfect world you would probably use the services of both professionals from day one, remember that you want these people working for you to give you every possible advantage in achieving financial success in your business.

When choosing a financial planner, adopt the same strategy as you would for finding any professional adviser. Ask friends and business associates for their recommendations. When meeting potential financial planners, ask for the names of several clients whom you could call to verify their abilities. If they aren't prepared to do this, look somewhere else.

11 **What to do if you get into financial trouble**

There are two types of businesses: those that have been short of cash and those that will be short of cash. I have yet to meet a self-made business person who hasn't had this problem at some time in their career.

How you handle difficult times is very important. You want people to continue to work with you and not immediately stop supplying you, which will ultimately close your business. In my early business days I made plenty of mistakes and was often short of cash. My response was to use the old 'the cheque's in the mail' routine, acting surprised when an angry supplier rang to say that they hadn't received payment.

Thanks to a kindly bank manager who sat me down one day and told me how to handle problems like mine, I discovered that there is a better way to handle this situation. Talk to people. If you let them know what is happening, why it is happening, and most importantly, what you are doing about it, most suppliers will bend over backwards to help you. They don't want to lose the money that you already owe them, and they certainly don't want to lose your business.

Working out a payment plan is a logical step. Some companies organise a system where you pay for all new orders up-front and pay off the outstanding amount over a set period of time. Whatever the arrangement, you work things out to the benefit of everyone.

There are also businesses that specialise in what is called turnaround management. They help businesses by talking to suppliers on your behalf. They can mediate with landlords and financial institutions, possibly help with restructuring your debt, and generally remove a lot of the pressure during these difficult times. These services aren't free; in fact, they can be quite costly. However, they can make the situation more bearable so that you can get on with the job at hand, boosting your business.

Apart from communication, the best way to handle and survive this situation is to avoid it. If you are concerned about the financial state of your business, talk to your accountant immediately. Once again, you have to be completely honest and open; half-truths will only hurt you more. I believe that more businesses go broke because of embarrassment than any other reason. By the time the business operator finally goes to talk to their accountant, it's often too late.

12 The real cost of expanding—can you afford it?

Expansion costs money. It's as simple as that, and there are plenty of businesses that have gone broke because they have expanded too quickly.

I have a friend who is a photographer and publisher. He runs an extremely successful and profitable business. I remember talking to him one day about how well his business was going. He looked me in the eye and said that he had to be very careful because his rapid expansion was making things very difficult financially. I was shocked and didn't really understand, until he explained that every time he expanded his products into a new business it cost him several thousand dollars in set-up costs and then he had extra outlays with maintaining his customer base.

Because his products were in such large demand, he had lots of shops that wanted to sell his books. It was nothing for him to have 50 or 60 new customers per month, which in reality cost him almost $150,000 to set up. It would take up to a year to recoup that money, so it's easy to see the burden that this kind of expansion would have on the company's cash flow. Luckily, he is a smart operator and he employed a good financial controller to help steer the company through the ongoing expansion.

There is a general philosophy that businesses should be growing and expanding all the time. It's important to understand that there is a cost to pay for this expansion and that you really need to plan your business's growth carefully, at a rate that you can afford.

Of course, for many businesses there are cost advantages to expanding, such as increased buying power. My point is that to get to that stage costs money, and your business needs to be able to afford the growth.

Another friend of mine, who owned a large transport company, always said that it was much harder to downsize a company than to expand. The point that he was making is that when you expand, you are basing the expansion on increasing revenue from more customers. If, for some reason, that suddenly stops, it's very hard on everyone to shrink the business down to a profitable level. Staff have to be laid off, office size reduced, debt decreased, and so on.

The main point of this booster tip is that if your business is growing due to demand, that's great. But be careful about how you manage that growth, and build into your business plan the fact that one day you might need to downsize.

13 **Beware of giving credit**

We all want customers, and we generally want lots of them. In our haste to build up a customer base, our credit control can often go out the window. I have owned several businesses that have nearly been sent broke because people wouldn't pay their accounts. I don't blame them; I blame myself for not being tougher about giving them credit in the first place.

At the end of the day, if *I* don't get paid, I can't pay other people. It's the classic vicious cycle that is very common in business. If you run a business where people pay you on the spot, you are one of the lucky ones. If you run a business in an industry that generally works on invoices and accounts, you need to be very careful.

The point of this survival tip is to be careful about giving out credit in an attempt to win the business. Of course, the majority of businesses are excellent at paying their accounts. They are not the ones to worry about. It's the others who are slow, or perhaps not trading very well, who are the concern.

If you give credit, you should have a system in place to check the applicant to make sure that they are good at paying their bills. Even the smallest business can have a credit check system in place. A simple form asking for several trade references is really all you need. (See the appendix at the back of this book for a sample credit request form.) Many companies now ask for a director of the company to sign a guarantee. It's up to you.

If we are approached by a new client for credit, we ask for several trade references and we always check them. We also ask other business associates if they know of the client and if they know much about them. If they check out, we will extend credit. If they don't check out, we ask for payment up-front. We generally ask for a 50 per cent deposit from all new clients as a matter of course to ensure that costs are covered.

Another important issue with extending credit is to ensure that your payment terms are clearly explained. If you are issuing a 30-day account, spell this out. If it's a seven-day account, make sure that the customer knows and acknowledges the fact. They may not be able to work to such a short payment time (often the case with large companies), so you will need to make another arrangement. Frank, open discussions about money and payment terms in the early stages of a business relationship will avoid problems in the future.

Another important point is that a company may be trading well when you start working together; they pay their bills on time and everything is fine. Then they start slowing down and 30 days turns into 60 days, and 60 into 90. Be aware that this is a warning signal that there may be a problem and you need to communicate with them to ensure that your money is safe.

Some businesses, when they have their credit cut, change suppliers. A good tip that I have read in the past is that if you suddenly get a new customer for no apparent reason, be careful that it isn't because no one else will give them credit.

14 Chasing bad debts—is it worth it?

If you are in the unfortunate situation of having bad debts that are long overdue and need chasing, you need to decide when to stop chasing them and when to write them off. Obviously, it's better not to have bad debts in the first place, and a good credit control system will, to a large degree, eliminate this problem.

Chasing bad debts costs time and money, sometimes a lot of both. I once owned a publication that was owed a lot of money, in excess of $50,000, that was long overdue. The business had struggled for a long time because credit was given too easily. It reached a point where the viability of the business was doubtful because this outstanding money couldn't be collected.

As I wasn't getting any results, I employed a debt collection agency. While they managed to get some money in, the vast majority was still outstanding. I was incurring costs all the time, and eventually the debt, with collection costs, was actually growing. Some of the companies that owed money went broke and I ended up recovering only a few cents in the dollar. Others were taken to court and judgments were received against the businesses but I still had to chase them for the money.

In reality, it was a joke. The majority of the money wasn't collected; in fact, I was almost $20,000 worse off due to collection fees, wages and telephone, stationery and other costs. This doesn't even take into consideration my time and the stress that the whole situation caused. I made the decision to write off the debts that couldn't be collected, and I have to admit that this was a very hard decision to take. If I didn't write them off I could still be chasing half of them today, and imagine how much they would have cost me then!

The moral to the story is to know when to say, 'Enough is enough'. As much as it might really aggravate you, there is a time when you have to let go of a debt and use it as a tax loss. This is particularly important when it comes to collecting small debts that can easily cost more to collect than the value of the debt. An associate of mine had worked out that it cost his company $100 per month to chase each outstanding account. Obviously, what for them was a small account of a few hundred dollars would soon be used up in collection costs.

If you are using a debt collection agency, make sure that you know exactly what steps they will take to recover your money and how much you are likely to be up for at every stage of the collection process. Getting a judgment in a court is no guarantee that you will get your money.

It's sometimes the case that people who owe you money are having legitimate problems and I would always say that it's better to work *with* these people and accept a payment plan, even if it's only a small amount per week or per month. By working with them you may get all of your money, and if their business turns around you may just end up with a very loyal client.

A friend of mine used to own a very seasonal business that sold gifts and souvenirs to tourists. In the peak of the season he had lots of cash flow, but in the off season he was always struggling. Over the years he had established a good rapport with his suppliers where for six months of the year he paid cash on delivery and for the other six months he paid in 90 days. This relationship worked for all parties and he always honoured his payments. His communication enabled him to work with his suppliers to ensure that his supply wasn't cut off in the off season, and they had a good customer who paid on the spot during the peak trading period. A situation like this is obviously a win–win, even if it is somewhat unconventional.

15 Keep good records from the start

If you are reading this book in the anticipation of opening your own business or buying a going concern, I cannot stress enough the importance of keeping good records from day one. There is really no other way to know how your business is going except by having good records.

If you are wondering where you put your cheque book, or that garbage bag in which you've stuffed the last five years worth of receipts—don't worry, it's never too late. Pay a book-keeper to get your records in order. It's not that expensive and it really is worth the effort.

There is something very satisfying in being able to press a few buttons on a computer and know exactly how much you owe, how much is owed to you and how much profit you have made so far this year. The only way you are able to know this is by keeping good records.

Taxation systems throughout the world are forcing business operators to keep better records, and while it can be time consuming it really isn't all that difficult. I know a number of people who don't pay themselves at the end of the week until they have brought their books up to date, or they pay themselves a bonus when they have done their books. Whatever works for you is fine.

Often the biggest problem with book work is where to put it. There are receipts, bank statements, cheque stubs, invoices, statements, and countless other bits and pieces. If you are not an organised person, you may need to find someone who can sort out your books for you.

I have a bookkeeper who comes in once a month. They spend five or six hours keying in the information, and at the end of the session I am given a profit and loss statement. This costs me around $200 per month. For the peace of mind it gives me this is a small price to pay.

16 Keeping costs down without losing customers

I often see companies that are going through difficult financial times trying to cut costs. The problem is that the areas where they are cutting costs are causing them to lose customers. This clearly compounds the problem and sends the business into a downward spiral.

It is smart business to keep your costs down as much as possible. There aren't too many businesses that couldn't shave thousands of dollars off their yearly operating costs by making a few simple changes or reviewing a few operational procedures.

It is important to think long and hard about the areas where cost cuts are to be made. Unfortunately, staff are normally the first to go, followed closely by advertising and marketing. These are often big expenses and they appear to be areas where cost savings can be made quickly.

Of course, dropping staff numbers can lead to customers having to wait longer, phones not being answered, orders not being processed, and so on. While there is no doubt that businesses sometimes become too staff heavy, it's essential that the level of customer service be monitored when changes are made to ensure that you don't start losing business as a result of your cost cuts.

With advertising and marketing, there is absolutely no doubt in my mind that the time you need to promote your business the most is when you are quiet. Advertising and marketing can take time to begin to have an effect. If you stop advertising altogether, you can compound your problem.

The point behind this booster tip is the need to plan your cost cutting; don't just be reactive.

17 How to know what to charge

One of the hardest issues that all business operators face is knowing how much to charge. If your prices are too high you might not get any customers, and if your prices are too low you might get a lot of customers but make no money. It's a fine line that is often hard to determine.

There is a basic business practice which, if followed, will make determining your costs a lot easier. First, you need to know how much it costs to run your business (see Booster Tip #6). Second, you need to decide how much you want to make out of your business. Add this to your costs and you will come up with a figure that determines how much money you need to make each hour, day, week, month and year.

From here you can generally determine an hourly rate, or the number of items that you need to sell at a certain price to meet your targets. Once you have determined this rate or price, do some homework. Check the prices of other businesses to see how much they are charging for similar products or services. If your sums are right you should be in the ballpark.

There are also some other factors to take into consideration. If your business is brand-new, you are an unknown quantity— you have no customers to serve as testimonials or references, so prospective customers have to assess you based on what you tell them and the prices that you charge. If your prices are too high with nothing to back them up, you might be looking for trouble.

On the other hand, if you have been in business for a while you will have a track record, happy customers, and experience that has a certain value. Based on this you can afford to charge more because you are a known quantity that can back up any promises that you make.

It is common for business operators to undercharge. I know that as consumers we always feel that we are being overcharged, but in reality it's often the other way around. Many business operators undervalue their own time and expertise.

My advice is to charge what you are worth. As long as you can deliver what you promise, you should be fine. It's also much harder to put prices up than it is to lower them. I'm not saying that you should rip people off—in fact, the exact opposite: give people value for their money and they will be prepared to pay for it.

Winning business or customers on price alone is hard work, and there are many, many examples of companies that haven't thrived using this principle. Determine what to charge based on your costs, your desired profits, the competition and your unique business features.

18 Don't invest your superannuation in a business venture

At various times in our lives, we may come into some money. It may be a superannuation payout, an inheritance from a relative, a redundancy package, share dividends or even a lottery win. Many people use these windfalls either to start their own business or to buy an existing one. Unfortunately, many of them soon lose this money.

One of the biggest areas of complaint in our lives is work. It stinks, the boss is a jerk and the pay is lousy. We have all heard it a hundred times, and we have all been in the same situation ourselves. Because of this perception, one of our biggest desires is to work for ourselves so that we never have to deal with a jerk of a boss again. When that big payout comes through, often the first thing we plan to do is buy a business where we will be our own boss.

This is where the problem begins, and I have started to see it happen more often in recent years. People with money, but no skills in running their own business, invest hundreds of thousands of dollars into a business and then lose the lot. Just because you have eaten at a restaurant five times a week for the past 20 years doesn't mean you can run one.

Now, don't get me wrong. I am an eternal optimist who encourages people to succeed wherever possible. But it breaks my heart to see a couple in their sixties have to go back into the workforce because they have lost their house or their superannuation payout on a business venture that was doomed from the start.

If you have a large chunk of money, or you are going to come into a large chunk of money, think long and hard about what you want to do with it. Running your own business isn't easy. It certainly doesn't mean freedom and can be more stressful than working for someone else.

On the other hand, it can be incredibly rewarding and satisfying and it is the life that many of us have chosen. However, we often go into business because we are in the field already. I was a sales and marketing manager for a large company, so it made sense for me to become a marketing consultant. If a mechanic working in a garage decides to start his own similar business, that makes sense to me. But a librarian deciding to start a fireworks company somehow doesn't.

By no means is this an all-encompassing rule—if it was, no innovative businesses would ever get off the ground—but it's the norm, rather than the exception. Before you part with your windfall, think long and hard about the good and the bad points of owning and running your own business. Don't get caught up in the idealistic daydream that few businesses offer in reality. Go into any business venture with your eyes wide open.

19 Beware the third-year boom and fourth-year bust

An unusual business phenomenon that I have been told about is the third-year boom and fourth-year bust. Once I became aware of it, I started to notice how real it was. The first year of business is generally pretty hard but exciting. It's the year where you jump for joy when you get your first customer or the first big contract and at the same time bite your nails wondering how to pay the electricity bill. It's a year that goes by quickly because there is so much happening.

Assuming that you have made it through the first year, the second year starts and you are a lot smarter. You have made a few mistakes, lost some money, done some great work and some that you might like to forget. Financially it's still hard, but you can see light at the end of the tunnel. Towards the end of the second year you start to notice that there is always a little more money left in the bank account at the end of the week, and you seem to be getting more and more customers because word of mouth is starting to spread about just how wonderful your business is. At the same time, you are tired and stressed because it's been a hard two years.

You are into the third year and business starts to boom. At the end of the week there is a lot of money left in the account and you can now start to reward yourself. Perhaps you buy yourself a new car, maybe even a new house, maybe a good holiday. While you are busy spending this money, phone calls aren't being returned, customers are starting to leave, bills aren't getting paid and you don't notice.

As you start the fourth year, your attention is shockingly brought back to the business when the tow truck pulls away with your shiny new sports car. At about the same time, the bank rings to say that your cheques are bouncing and finally you are forced to close the doors.

I'm not saying that every business goes through this cycle, but if you keep an eye out you will notice that it happens a lot. Being aware of it may help you to avoid it.

Notes

....
....
....
....
....
....
....
....
....
....
....
....
....
....
....
....
....

Booster Tips Action List

Things to do   **Completed**

1. ....
2. ....
3. ....
4. ....
5. ....
6. ....
7. ....
8. ....
9. ....
10. ....

4 | Business relationship booster tips

In business we form relationships with many different people. These relationships are on a number of different levels, requiring the average business person to change hats regularly throughout the working day. The relationship you will have with your staff is different from the relationship you will have with your bank manager or with your customers. Each is important, but they have fundamental differences that, once identified, tend to make the process of relationship building much easier.

In the end, the better your relationship is with everyone you deal with, the better off you will be. Life will be simpler, there will be fewer conflicts, and you will be able to focus on what you do best.

The ideas we'll talk about in this section are:

#20 Partnership pitfalls—how to avoid them
#21 Build a relationship with your suppliers
#22 Build a relationship with your landlord
#23 Build a relationship with your professional advisers
#24 Build a relationship with people in your industry
#25 Find a balance between work and home
#26 Use mediation to solve conflict
#27 Accept that others may not share your enthusiasm

20 Partnership pitfalls—how to avoid them

Having a partner in business can be both a blessing and a disaster. The sad reality is that partnerships have a high rate of failure, due to problems between the partners themselves and not with the business. I have had several partnerships, but only one that has really worked. In that case, the partners were silent and very supportive.

The biggest problem with partnerships is that the partners spend a lot of time planning the honeymoon and no time planning the divorce. What I mean by this is that one day, you may find that your business partner is driving you crazy and you no longer want to be involved with them. If you have a written plan and agreement on what to do in this situation, you just pull it out and implement it; it's like a business pre-nuptial agreement. If you *don't* have an agreement, though, things can suddenly turn ugly.

I mentioned earlier in this book the importance of setting realistic goals and budgets. If you have a partner, there is always a chance that the relationship simply won't work—regardless of how close you are as friends or relatives today. If it reaches the stage when you need to part company (and you will know that time when it arrives), you need to have what is commonly known as an exit strategy. This is simply a plan that outlines how you or your partner can get out of the business with minimal damage and loss.

I strongly recommend that you budget some money when setting up your business to have a lawyer draw up a partnership dissolution agreement, which is the legal form for an exit strategy. It is in both your and your partner's interests to have such an agreement. It is important that all parties are fully aware of what it means and the implications of signing it. Basically, an exit strategy document normally allows the remaining partner the first option to buy out the departing partner at a price determined in a pre-agreed manner.

I have painted a pretty grim picture of partnerships, and you may now be looking across your desk at your partner with some trepidation. However, like any relationship, a successful business partnership can also be very emotionally and financially rewarding. It's all about communication and working together. If you are lucky enough to have a strong partnership, congratulations; if you are involved in an awkward partnership, try to work things out.

My pool of advisers all made the same comment: partners are often a necessary evil. You may need their money, their expertise, or a combination of the two. Ensure that everything is in writing and plan for the day that you hope never comes.

21 Build a relationship with your suppliers

Suppliers are an important part of any business. Having a good relationship with your suppliers will help you to get through the hard times. Most relationships with suppliers start off somewhat tenuously, with both parties kind of checking each other out. How you treat your suppliers will play a big part in how they treat you.

I often hear people complaining about how slack their suppliers are about this or that; about how they are unreliable and always letting them down. Sometimes I find this quite amusing, as I have seen the same companies doing the same things to their own customers.

Like any relationship it needs to be built on solid foundations. If you become known for always phoning up to complain, your suppliers will soon become sick and tired of hearing from you. Be professional and courteous, and try to develop a rapport with individuals within the company. It's much easier if you can give Steve, the sales manager, a call and ask him to courier you an urgently needed part as a personal favour, rather than have to go through a sea of anonymous faces who will probably say 'no' as a reflex action.

Likewise, if you are having a lean month and cash is short, your suppliers need to be on side. If you are a bad payer, they may not want to deal with you anymore. If it's just a temporary situation and you have a good relationship with your suppliers, business will likely proceed as usual. You need your suppliers, and they need you. Why not work together and make everyone's life a little easier?

I had a client who always required their printing done urgently. Every job was desperately urgent, and I had to pass this message on to the printers. However, when every order was urgent, the printers stopped treating them as such. Then when I really *did* need another job done urgently, it was a struggle to get the printers to take me seriously. I had to sit down and explain to the client that they needed either to review their ordering timing, or to order larger quantities to help alleviate the problem they were inadvertently causing.

Now I ask my clients for realistic deadlines for their printing requirements. I mark the job accordingly, and I have a contract with my printer that states that they will do everything in their power to complete the jobs according to my deadline. Where possible I allow as much time as I can, and the really urgent jobs now get done very quickly. Everyone wins.

A lot of people use the word 'urgent' on orders, telephone messages and emails. Only do this if it really *is* urgent, otherwise people will stop taking you seriously and the last people you want in this category are your suppliers.

22 Build a relationship with your landlord

Love them or hate them, landlords play a big part in any business. If you are planning on buying a business or renting a space, do a little homework first on the landlord.

I once had an office that had communal toilets shared by six other businesses. As public toilets, it was up to the landlord to clean and maintain them. We received a letter one day saying that as a group we were using too much toilet paper and from now on we would have to supply our own. This, of course, was ridiculous and led me to ask the landlord if we were supposed to hand our clients a roll of toilet paper on their way to the toilet.

If you have a good relationship with your landlord, your business life will be made much easier. Our business is located in a high-rise building owned by a prominent Japanese company. I had heard all sorts of rumours about how difficult the company could be, so it was with a degree of trepidation that I started negotiations for renting an office. From day one, the company and their representatives were fantastic—100 per cent supportive, friendly, pleasant to deal with and understanding. They even sent me flowers during a recent stay in hospital, and now our company works on a lot of their property marketing projects. It's a two-way street. We pay our rent on time (well, most of the time) and we spent a lot of money fitting out our offices. We attract customers to the building and have added an air of professionalism to a part of the building that was rundown and starting to look empty.

In another case I have been evicted at short notice because I didn't have a legal lease, only a simple letter of intent, and the landlord wanted the space for themselves. This very traumatic and expensive experience highlighted the importance of having a lawyer read over any lease documents.

It's essential that you know and understand your rights as a tenant. My latest lease document is over 100 pages in length, with so many clauses and techno-legal talk that most people would have no chance of understanding it. While there was nothing intentionally wrong with the lease, my lawyer identified a number of points that could have been of concern down the line. By spending $500 to have the lease reviewed, I was reassured and my landlords made several amendments that kept us both happy.

There are many organisations that can offer excellent advice on your legal rights as a tenant, and if you need help a quick surf on the Internet will find the names and contact details for these organisations. As always, prevention is better than a cure, so ensure that all of your homework and legal advice is completed before you even think about signing a lease document.

Your landlord has a vested interest in your business succeeding. It means that they get a rent cheque each month. If you go broke, no one wins. I strongly suggest that you do your best to work together as a team. It also pays to shop around when it comes to leasing a premises. Everything is negotiable to a degree, and even if your landlord won't negotiate on the rental price, perhaps there are other areas where they can be more accommodating.

23 Build a relationship with your professional advisers

I encourage everyone reading this book to use professional advisers, including accountants, financial advisers and solicitors. In fact, I believe strongly that you should call in professional advice whenever you need help outside your field of experience. Most importantly, do it as soon as possible; don't wait for the problem to get worse before calling in the cavalry.

Building a relationship with your professional advisers is important. Don't just look at them as people who are billing you by the hour. Where possible, get to know them and how they think. In Asian cultures, a lot of time is spent getting to know people. A friend of mine is currently working in Korea, setting up a large aquarium. He has travelled a lot, and conducted many sales trips to Korea in the past but had very little success. Having now spent some time there, he has realised that it's all about building relationships. Koreans like to get to know you before doing business with you. In the past, my friend would try to visit as many companies as possible; now he realises that his time would have been better spent visiting just one company on each trip, spending as much time as possible getting to know the key people and letting them get to know him.

As someone who charges by the hour and falls into the category of a professional adviser, I have to say that I am fussy about who I do business with. If I don't like a particular person or business, I will do my utmost to avoid working for them. All of my clients are friends, and while I don't socialise with them a lot I would go out of my way to help them in any way I could and I know they would do the same for me.

Treat your professional advisers as people. Odds on they won't bill you for all the work they actually do, and if they like you, the ink will normally be a little lighter on the invoice. Develop a long-term relationship with your advisers and make sure that they know where you are going and the role that you want them to play in getting you there.

24 Build a relationship with people in your industry

There are two distinct groups within most industries: those who are willing to share information; and those who want to guard everything, treating all knowledge as top secret. From my experience those who are willing to share information often end up being far more successful because they get back as much information as they give out.

I am a firm believer in exchanging information. It can be very beneficial to talk to other industry associates who are open-minded to see if they share your thoughts on current industry trends, new methods, new products, and so on. This is, after all, what makes any industry grow and expand.

I work very hard to establish a strong rapport with my industry peers. This is made somewhat easier by the fact that I live in a small regional city, because I tend to know the other players through the course of my everyday business dealings. In larger cities it can be harder, but often industry groups are more organised, with larger member bases, allowing for more functions, meetings and conventions.

Working with your industry peers enables you to share your successes and failures. If you can share an experience that helps to prevent an industry associate from making the same mistake, you are doing more than a good deed; you are establishing your own credibility as a professional.

It's also a great feeling to be able to sit down with your peers, regardless of whether you are a florist or a flautist, and be able to openly discuss problems that you may be experiencing. It's reassuring to know that you are not the only one having these problems (and the chances are that you're not).

Successful business boosters aren't afraid to be open and frank with their industry peers. They may keep specific details close to their chest (which I agree with), but they are secure enough in their own abilities to be willing participants in a fair exchange of information.

25 Find a balance between work and home

This is a tough one on many fronts. To boost your business, you need to be able to work enough to keep the wolves at bay and relax enough to keep the family remembering your name. Most business people have trouble finding a balance between the two.

I have a tendency to be a workaholic and it's only when I arrive home and find several suitcases sitting by the front door that I realise I have been neglecting my family and I had better do something about it. Often the problem can be rectified with some simple time management training (see Booster Tip #115), but it's also a matter of establishing priorities.

When you are caught up in your own business it's very exciting. You enjoy spending time doing all of the little things that make you feel like it's your own business. Sometimes just sitting in your shop or office after hours can be quite inspirational, but the problem is that work soon takes over and we launch into the standard excuse, 'I need to work this hard to cover my bills.'

I realised one day that I didn't *have* to work the long hours I was working, that I actually *enjoyed* the feeling of martyrdom that many small business owners experience. I liked to moan about how hard things were and how hard I had to work, and to have other small business owners nod their heads in understanding. It's a load of codswallop. The problem with most of us is that we work long hours but we don't know how to work efficiently, so half the day is wasted. As a result, we have to work every weekend to catch up. And while we lament having to work yet another weekend, our small business friends are patting us on the back saying they understand how tough it is.

I know that there are times when money is tight. Sitting in the workshop and cleaning the spanners at midnight isn't going to help. In fact, it will do more harm than good. If you are going to thrive in business, you need to learn to be efficient with your time and to work smarter.

Don't try to win the martyr of the month award—go for the efficiency award instead. Most of the successful people I know work relatively short hours—they work when they want, they earn more as they get older, and they know how to enjoy themselves. I very rarely hear them complaining about how hard they are working. They all understand the martyrdom rollercoaster ride and have learned to outgrow it and to change the perception that, because you work for yourself, you have to work a hundred hours per week.

If you are to last in business and boost your business, you will need to learn how to work smarter and to balance your home life with your work life. Make sure that your goals include personal goals as well as business goals.

26 Use mediation to solve conflict

We all have to deal with conflict in our businesses. It can be from an unhappy customer, a disgruntled employee, the land-lord, someone you owe money to, a partner, or someone who is taking legal action against you. Dealing with conflict can be very distressing, and unless you know how to do it the results can be anything from poor to disastrous.

A lot of legal firms now use professional mediators to help resolve deadlocked disputes. This is done to free up the courts, which are slowly being jammed by tens of thousands of relatively minor law suits that should never have got as far as a courtroom.

The aim of mediation is simple: to try and get both parties to negotiate and settle their dispute without incurring extra costs and wasting more time. For mediation to be successful, both parties have to agree to treat the mediator as impartial and to listen to their advice. The mediator's role is to find a resolution that is as close to fair for both parties as possible.

Mediation isn't an easy road, but it's far easier and far less expensive than going to court. With mediation both sides win and both sides lose, to varying degrees. With court proceedings, one side wins and one side loses. It's great if you win, but not so great if you lose. Even if you win, it's often hardly worth it because of the legal expenses that cannot be recouped, the time lost and the stress.

Mediation can be used on a smaller scale in the workplace. If you have a problem that needs resolving with a member of staff, try to find someone who will act as a mediator for you. It's important that this person is deemed acceptable by both parties—you can't just announce that your brother Bill is going to mediate whether the other party likes it or not.

Mediation is a form of respect. By showing respect for the other party, half the battle is won. You are saying that you hear their grievance and understand that it's important to them and, as a result, that it's important to you, important enough to seek mediation.

Many retired politicians are going into this field. I don't know if this is a good advertisement for mediators or not, but there is no doubt in my mind that mediation can solve a lot of problems and let you get on with the task at hand. The two main factors to remember with this booster tip are to resolve conflict as quickly as possible (the longer battles go on, the worse they become), and be prepared to negotiate to solve the problem. No one wins a long, drawn-out argument or conflict.

27 Accept that others may not share your enthusiasm

This may seem a strange subject for a booster tip, but it's meant to point up the fact that there are many aspects to boosting your business, not just profit and loss statements.

We can all get a little carried away when we become a business owner. We love what we do and we become very excited about it. I have a friend who sells plants around the world. He is so passionate about it that the minute you mention anything to do with plants, his eyes light up and his enthusiasm takes fire. I find the business side of what he does fascinating; however, others could easily find it boring. I could (and do) talk marketing all day long. I love it. Most people have limited tolerance and normally I can tell when they have reached their boredom threshold. It doesn't mean that they are not interested in what we do; it just means that they are not as interested as we are. You need to accept the fact that other people may not be doing handstands every time you get a new customer.

Recently I got a phone call from my publisher saying that 10,000 copies of my first book were going to be translated and printed in China. I was doing cartwheels. The team in the office all said, 'That's great, but what are we going to do about the newspaper advertisement for a client that needs to be in by 2.30 p.m., and the market research campaign that's due to start tomorrow and we haven't finalised the questionnaire?' My elation lasted about 30 seconds and then it was back to business. At first I was a little hurt by this, but then I realised that while my team were extremely happy about my success, at the moment they had other things to deal with that were more important to them. On their way out of the office at the end of the day, everyone made a point of coming over and congratulating me.

Accept that not everyone will share your passion for and enthusiasm about what you do, or experience your trials and tribulations the way you do. What is important to remember is that you shouldn't take it personally. You are your own product champion, and no one will ever get as excited as you. Thriving in business means not getting upset or offended when others don't share your enthusiasm.

Notes

....
....
....
....
....
....
....
....
....
....
....
....
....
....
....
....

Booster Tips Action List

Things to do	Completed
1.	....
2.	....
3.	....
4.	....
5.	....
6.	....
7.	....
8.	....
9.	....
10.	....

5 | Staff booster tips

I tend to get a little brassed off when people complain about their staff, though I have been guilty of the same crime myself on a number of occasions. Most of the time the problem isn't with the staff, it's with us. Perhaps we have simply employed the wrong person for the job, or put a person in a job and given them no training to enable them to do their work properly.

This section looks at ways to boost your business by preventing these mistakes from happening. It also deals with the issues of motivation and communication and ways to encourage your staff to perform at their best.

The ideas we'll talk about in this section are:

#28 Put the job description in writing
#29 Always check references
#30 A trial period protects both you and the new employee
#31 Train your staff (and yourself) properly
#32 Lead by example and your team will follow
#33 Communicate effectively with your staff
#34 Conduct performance reviews
#35 Be conscious of security issues—protect your business
#36 Dismiss staff who don't work out
#37 Balance your staff numbers

28 Put the job description in writing

Very few businesses take the time to write a position description for each member of staff. This is typically a brief document that outlines the employer's expectations of their new recruit. The hard work is normally in writing the first position description. After that, it can be adapted to suit other positions as required. The type of information that can be included varies from business to business. Typically, the following information is included:

- The company's general philosophy and mission statement to ensure that the employee understands where you are coming from.
- What the employee is expected to do and when they should have it done by. This ensures that everyone is clear about the job and all that it entails.
- Exactly what the employee receives for doing the job. This should include how much they will be paid, the number of days allowed for annual holidays and sick days, the company's contribution to superannuation, and other items such as medical insurance, maternity/paternity leave and any performance-based incentives. This section should also include any other form of remuneration for the employee, including such things as the supply of uniforms, free parking, length of breaks, and so on.
- Company policies—this section enables you to detail your company policy on issues that may be relevant to the new employee. It can cover everything from staff discounts, to dealing with complaints with other staff, security, insurance, and so on.
- General housekeeping issues—what time they are expected to start and finish work, how they should dress, how they should deal with other members of staff, notice period required for resigning, when they will be paid and how, and so on.

The position description should be read and signed by the new employee and they should be given a copy for their own records. It protects both you and them. If you are uncertain about any aspect of the document, get your legal representative to have a look at it. Many business advisory boards will have standard forms that enable you just to fill in the blanks.

Use the position description to start the relationship off on a professional level. Disputes that arise between staff and management simply because there is nothing in writing can be very costly in terms of time and lost productivity, and often lead to resentment.

It's also a very good idea to review the position description with your staff periodically. This ensures that everyone is up to date and that any potential problems are addressed (see also Booster Tip #34).

29 Always check references

Most businesses will employ people at some stage. There are a number of ways you can go about finding people to work for you. Some organisations like to use an employment agency to make the process less cumbersome. It's then up to the agency to find suitable applicants that they feel will meet your requirements. Of course, you pay for this service, but it can save you a lot of time.

If you employ people by placing your own advertisements, you will probably be used to receiving lots of résumés. I have yet to see a résumé that isn't impressive; after all, that's the whole idea of sending them out. The problem is, just because someone says that they are great, it doesn't mean they are.

I always check references. While the majority of people are very honest, some are not. Often past employers are surprised to find that they have been included as a reference, and they may tell a very different story about the applicant and their abilities.

I have agreed to be a reference for about 20 people during my working career. I have only ever been contacted twice to verify the abilities of the people I have recommended. It's surprising to me that more employers don't check references. They often employ people based only on what is written in the résumé and a brief interview.

When checking references, ask detailed questions and make sure that the facts add up. Don't just ring the referee and ask if the person worked for them. Ask them if there were any problems. Tell them about your business and what you do. Do they think that the applicant will work well and produce results for your business?

Another point worth noting here is that if you agree to act as a reference for a former employee, be honest if someone contacts you to check on them. This honesty should extend to both the person's good points and bad points.

30 A trial period protects both you and the new employee

It is an excellent idea to put new staff on a trial period when they start working for you. This may be a few weeks, or a few months, depending on the complexity of the job. The duration of the trial period should be made very clear to all applicants and should be included in the position description (see Booster Tip #28).

The whole idea of a trial period is to protect both you and the new employee. It is becoming harder and harder to terminate staff if they are not working out. If you have a clearly defined cooling-off period, you know that you have an out if you need one.

Likewise, an employee may find themselves in the job from hell, with a psychotic boss they cannot work with. A trial period removes any awkwardness and provides the employee with a simple explanation when they apply for future jobs. 'I worked for The Widget Company for a trial period of one month, but I felt that the work wasn't really challenging enough for me so I left at the end of the trial period to enable my employer to find someone better suited to the job.' This is a mature and responsible way to handle short-term periods of employment that haven't worked out.

I have to admit that I have hired people and not instigated a trial period, and I have really regretted it. Finding the right person for the right job is difficult at the best of times, and it's a simple fact of life that sometimes the first person you employ simply doesn't work out. Provide yourself with a back-door exit clause by having a trial period.

31 Train your staff (and yourself) properly

This is a bit of bugbear for me. I often see inadequately trained staff being blamed for poor performance simply because their boss wouldn't pay for training. If you expect someone to do a job properly, you need to give them the necessary skills.

I believe that many businesses look at new staff as an inconvenience, rather than as a promising opportunity to boost the business. This is often true in larger organisations, where lots of people come and go on a regular basis.

If you are going to pay your staff every week, surely you want them to do the best job possible for you? After all, the better the job they do, the happier your customers will be and the more profit your business will make.

Training takes many shapes and forms. It's essential to train your new staff in how your business operates. They need to be made aware of your expectations and those of your customers. Every business is slightly different—even two virtually identical hamburger restaurants will have different operational procedures that staff need to be taught. Take the time to orientate new staff and train them fully so that they know how to do their job for you.

Another type of training covers general skills. This may include telephone manner, customer service, selling skills, and even things like time management. These general skills are used by most businesses, but for many people they don't come instinctively. Enrol your staff in a training course, or contract a trainer to come to your workplace to conduct in-house training. The cost will be covered by improved efficiency and a higher degree of customer satisfaction.

The third type of training covers specific skills that are relevant to your type of business or industry. People often choose to work for a particular company because it will give them the opportunity to learn new skills. Give your staff the skills to keep them at the forefront of your industry and you, and they, will reap the benefits.

Just as it is important for your staff to be well trained, don't forget to put your hand up from time to time to undergo training yourself. I haven't met anyone who couldn't benefit from some form of training. We all need to expand our skills and expertise. Often, when we find ourselves running a business, we know how to do our job very well, but we may not know how to do bookeeping work, how to manage our time or how to be a better negotiator.

Another common problem that I see with training is that organisations go through stages. They may have five training courses in one month and then nothing for the rest of the year. Try to plan your training so that it's conducted at frequent intervals throughout the year. I like to do training during non-productive times, when business tends to be quiet. Rather than having people sitting around doing crosswords have them learning new skills or improving existing skills.

There are many organisations that offer training. Some training is very expensive, while some is not. I recommend consulting your local business groups to find out what kind of training is available in your area. You may even be entitled to financial assistance for certain types of training. Spend a little time researching your training options before implementing a course of action.

Another smart business move that I have observed is to ask your staff what areas they feel they need training in. This can, of course, open a can of worms (you might not have the room to run synchronised swimming classes), but you might be surprised by the types of things they want to learn.

We have done a number of surveys for organisations asking this exact question, and I have been surprised by the responses. Two of the main areas that people appear to want help with are stress management and dealing with change in the workplace. Both are clearly reflections of the modern-day working environment.

32 Lead by example and your team will follow

If you turn up for work in a pair of shorts and a T-shirt, yet you expect your staff to wear Armani suits, you are asking for trouble. If you take long lunches every day and complain when your staff are a couple of minutes late after a break, you are sending conflicting messages.

Your words and actions will determine the words and actions of your staff. If *you* work hard, *they* will work hard. If *you* are polite and friendly, *they* will be polite and friendly. If *you* are less than honest, *they* will be less than honest. It is important to understand that, in your business, you set the ground rules that everyone plays by. Make them good rules and stick to them yourself, and you will reap the rewards.

33 Communicate effectively with your staff

Some people are good at communicating, while others are not. Having clear communication with your staff ensures that your business will run efficiently and effectively.

From my experience, there are two types of communicators: those that don't communicate at all; and those that bombard staff with memos, meetings and hundreds of other forms of communication. Somewhere in the middle is the best objective.

Often poor communicators simply don't know how to pass on information. There are several easy ways to do this:

1. *Staff meetings.* These should be held regularly, preferably at the same time each day, week or month, depending on your needs. They provide an open forum for information to be shared in both directions.

2. *A noticeboard.* This enables information to be passed on without disrupting normal work practices. Putting the noticeboard in an area where all staff have to go at some time during the day makes it easy for them to read the notices. I read about a company recently that put its notice-boards in the toilets, because it was the only place where all the staff visited during the course of the day.

3. *Memos.* These are normally one-page documents that are distributed to all staff with a specific point being the subject of the memo. The problem with memos is that often people don't read them. I suggest that memos should be signed when read and then passed on. This can, of course, be time consuming and not necessarily the best way to get a message across, but it's a tool that can be used.

4. *Email.* Intracompany email has become the quickest and most cost-effective way of passing on information within larger organisations. Unfortunately, because email is easy to send, it can be over-used. A friend of mine receives up to 100 inter-office emails every day, many of which aren't relevant to his work. I suspect that this is a common problem.

I am a verbal communicator, so I prefer to sit down and talk face-to-face with my team. You need to determine what works for you and what works for your business. The important point to take from this booster tip is that having an effective mechanism for dispersing information in your business will improve your chances of thriving.

34 Conduct performance reviews

In reality, jobs change and an individual's responsibilities can change during their period of employment. For this reason, position descriptions should be reviewed periodically. This process enables both parties to air any grievances or concerns they may have.

By conducting performance reviews, you are sending a clear message to your staff that they are expected to perform. Regular reviews can help to prevent non-performing staff from hiding among the crowd.

Depending on the size of your organisation, the performance review can be a formal process or a simple chat over a cup of coffee. However it's done, it should be documented and on file and a copy given to the employee.

As with many workplace issues, you may need to ask your legal adviser about the best way to conduct these meetings. I would recommend that you do this to ensure that you are covered legally. Often performance reviews require a third person to be present to act as a witness.

Have a simple agenda when doing a performance review. This can include:

- The employee's thoughts on how they are performing.
- Your thoughts on how the employee is performing.
- Identification of areas where the employee is doing well.
- Identification of areas that the employee needs to work on.
- The employee's goals and plans for their future involvement with your organisation.
- Your plans for the future of the employee.
- Review of the employee's responsibilities and pay structure, if applicable.
- An open session to air any problems or grievances.

This review period is also an excellent time to offer rewards for a job well done.

It may appear that all I am doing is creating more work. In reality, I am suggesting a way to increase the productivity of your staff. A harmonious workplace is much more likely to produce profits than a tense, aggressive environment where staff are constantly embroiled in internal politics. By being open and honest, you are sending a very clear message that you expect the same from them.

35 Be conscious of security issues—protect your business

I used to be a cynic when it came to security. After all, who would want any key information about a little marketing company like mine? I have since witnessed so many security breaches, not only of my business but also many of my clients', that I am no longer a cynic.

I can guarantee that your competitors would love to know your most intimate business secrets, even simple details like who your main customers are, who your key suppliers are, how much you charge, and so on. Of course, with a little investigative work it isn't hard to find this information, but there are people who will often give it out, sometimes innocently, without your knowledge.

Unfortunately, the Internet isn't only one of the greatest promotional tools, it's also one of the easiest ways to breach a company's security. While writing this book, I watched a documentary on television about Internet hackers and what they could achieve, and it was very, very frightening. If your computer is hooked up to a telephone line, you are at risk.

Of course, the big question is: what do you do about Internet security and security in general? If you have information that you absolutely don't want other people to know about, then don't put it on your computer. Produce a number of hard copies and then delete the file or store it on an external disk that you take with you. Computer security software and protective barriers such as firewalls are improving all the time. For most of our businesses they are more than sufficient; however, if you have any doubts, the only way to ensure that someone doesn't steal information from your computer is not to have it stored on the computer, or to use a computer that isn't connected to a network (other computers) or a telephone line. I know a number of business people who use a separate computer for their financial records that is completely password-protected and separate from all other computers and phone lines.

When it comes to other information that could either be stolen or passed on by staff, let them know what information can and cannot be freely given out. Once again, you are setting the ground rules by letting them know what is acceptable and what is not.

Staff theft is always an issue, and unfortunately it's becoming a greater problem for businesses. Staff often don't consider taking products home as theft; some see it as a benefit of the job. You need to set very clear boundaries and parameters for what staff can and cannot take or use, and you should make your views on, and the ramifications of, staff theft very clear. Grey areas invite theft and can cost your business a lot of money. Likewise, poor stock control invites theft, simply because you can't tell when things go missing.

Shoplifting is also a growing problem and one that any retail business needs to address. Store layout has a lot to do with shoplifting, and there are many things that can be done to minimise losses as a result of stealing. Shoplifters are organised, brash and very confident, and they often work in teams.

Many organisations use cameras. I don't like the idea of this myself, and in some instances it can be a real invasion of privacy; however, in other instances, such as late-night petrol stations and convenience stores, camera surveillance is essential.

If security is a real issue for you, get some advice from a specialist. There are plenty of companies that can help you develop your security to the level that you require.

It's often a good idea to talk to your insurance company about security as well. The cost of a specialist security consultant can often be recouped by reduced insurance policies for having a more secure premises.

36 Dismiss staff who don't work out

This is a tough one. No one likes to tell a member of staff that they are no longer required, and no one likes to hear those dreaded words.

I once had a publishing business that employed several sales representatives who sold advertising. One rep just wasn't working out. My partner and I tried everything, including sales training, motivation, money, begging—the lot. It was clear from day one that she was wrong for the position. On several occasions I started my 'I don't think this is working out' line, but I could never follow through. We made the decision that she had to go. The date was set and the appointment was made. In she came, a tiny girl in a big boardroom chair. My partner and I had steeled ourselves. This was the day; nothing was going to stop the inevitable. I started my 'I don't think this is working out' speech. Her bottom lip quivered, as did my nerve, but I kept going and just as I was about to say, 'Today is your last day', my partner rushed over and gave her a big hug and said: 'But don't worry, we're willing to keep trying.' Well, my jaw hit the ground. She stayed with us for several more months before finally leaving.

Let's be honest, sacking someone is the ultimate in rejection and people don't like it. There are times in any business when, for one reason or another, you will have to dismiss staff and I believe that people generally know when they are about to be laid off. It's important to have a clear process or procedure that you can use in this situation.

Check with your legal adviser to find out what your obligations are when it comes to terminating a member of staff. If you don't follow the appropriate steps, you may open yourself up for legal action in the future. I also feel that it's better to talk to someone face-to-face, rather than just drop them a DCM (don't come Monday) via their email.

I once met someone who had worked in a government organisation for 25 years. He found out that he was getting the sack from the pay department when he went to change his account details. The accounts clerk showed him a memo from management saying that he was being terminated. He was devastated and later successfully sued his former employer. I have also heard horror stories of staff being advised of their termination over the loudspeaker for all to hear.

How you go about terminating an employee is up to you, but do it legally, with dignity and with sensitivity.

37 Balance your staff numbers

Without doubt, staffing costs are one of the major overheads that businesses face. As soon as you start employing people, your weekly overheads go through the roof. Of course, most businesses cannot operate without staff, so you need to plan your employment well. The real art is learning to balance your staffing levels against the amount of work that needs to be done or the number of customers that need to be served. This skill normally evolves over time, but it's an area that needs to be constantly addressed and monitored.

Staff need to be paid at the end of the week. They have entitlements which you must legally adhere to, and you need to allow for the fact that extra staff means other additional costs, such as higher telephone charges, additional office equipment such as computers, uniforms, extra sets of tools, business cards, and often much more. Be certain to make a list of the added costs and when you will need to pay them, to ensure that your cash flow can afford more staff.

The use of casual or part-time staff is a great way to build up your workforce in a manner that works with your cash flow. We employ a lot of part-time telemarketers who work on various projects. Most of them have other jobs and work for our company to earn extra income. This isn't a new idea of course, but it's often a better way to go than employing full-time staff.

I have seen many businesses get themselves into trouble through having far too many staff for the amount of income they generate. Most businesses have busy periods and quiet periods, reinforcing the need for careful planning. Be cautious when employing new staff, and focus on making your staff as productive as possible.

Notes

....
....
....
....
....
....
....
....
....
....
....
....
....
....
....
....

Booster Tips Action List

Things to do   **Completed**

1. ....
2. ....
3. ....
4. ....
5. ....
6. ....
7. ....
8. ....
9. ....
10. ....

6 | Customer service booster tips

A theme repeated throughout this book is the need to respect consumers and your customers. This section identifies many of the common mistakes that businesses make when it comes to looking after their customers. It provides the basic steps that all businesses should adopt to ensure that they offer customer service that is better than their competitors'. It also looks at the right and wrong way to deal with customer complaints, the value of market research and how to apply it to your business, and a number of philosophies that should be avoided to prevent poor customer service.

The ideas we'll talk about in this section are:

#38 Build a relationship with your customers
#39 Learn to say 'no'
#40 Use simple market research to keep on track
#41 Continually ask your customers if they are happy
#42 Deliver what you promise—if you can't do this, get out of the game
#43 Be honest and upright in all your dealings
#44 The right and wrong way to handle a complaint
#45 Treat your customers with the respect that they deserve
#46 Learn to recognise when you need a break from your customers

38 Build a relationship with your customers

A lot of research has been done in recent years into the 'lifetime value' of customers. What this means is: look at your customers in broader terms than the purchase they are currently making. Larger corporations have realised that if they can keep their customers happy and satisfied for longer periods of time, they can increase their profits dramatically. This is based on the maxim that it costs a lot less to keep existing customers than it does to attract new ones.

The value of word-of-mouth advertising is also starting to be quantified. Organisations are now able to put a dollar value on the benefits of happy customers spreading the word (for free) about their business. Of course, this varies dramatically from business to business and industry to industry; however, we are all consumers and we have a lot of choice about when and where we want to spend our money.

Deciding where to spend is becoming harder as competition increases. One of the best ways to make this choice is to ask someone you trust for a recommendation. There wouldn't be too many people who don't ask their friends, family members or work colleagues for advice on where to buy certain products. Restaurants flourish or fail based on word-of-mouth recommendations. Mechanics, doctors, lawyers, hotels, fashion retailers, and just about every other industry, rely heavily on word-of-mouth referrals. My business is based almost 100 per cent on word-of-mouth recommendations, where my clients tell their friends and associates and they contact me to do work for them.

Based on this phenomenon, we all need to build strong, long-term relationships with our customers. All of our dealings and basic business philosophies need to be committed to the long-term benefits of keeping the customer coming back. It needs to be an accepted way of doing business in your organisation that the people you are dealing with today will still be coming back in ten years' time.

A big plus to building long-term customer relations is that you can spend a lot less money on advertising and marketing if all of your current customers are out there spreading the word about your wonderful business. It's really like having a team of sales reps without the cost of the salaries, cars and holidays, and other headaches.

39 Learn to say 'no'

Saying 'no' isn't as easy as it sounds. A lot of people have trouble saying this simple word, often out of a fear of offending or upsetting another person. All of the successful business people I spoke to while researching this book had the ability to say this magic word when necessary.

There are many situations when we need to be able to say 'no' on a daily basis, such as when someone is trying to sell us something that we really can't afford, when we are being pressured by someone to do something that we don't agree with or we feel can't be done in the time allowed, or even when we haven't the time to meet with someone.

I believe that we are taught from an early age that it's rude to say 'no'. I know that I struggled for many years with saying 'no' to people. The consequence of this was that I never had any time to myself, I took on jobs that I really didn't want to do, I dealt with people I didn't really like, and I struggled to get by because I was over-committed in so many areas of my life.

I have since learned how to say 'no' to people, and I believe that to be successful at this task you need to practise it. If you can't say 'no', your chances of success are reduced, because your time will be spent doing things that you resent rather than those things you want and perhaps need to be doing.

I also believe that there are both good and bad ways to say 'no'. While you don't want to offend anyone, you should be able to make your own decisions; if someone doesn't like the outcome, that's their problem, not yours.

There may be times when you are being pressured by a customer into supplying a particular product or service by an unrealistic deadline. I have made a conscious effort to explain to my clients when I can do a particular job by. I pride myself on doing work of a very high standard, and if I can't meet their deadline I will offer advice on other ways to meet their demands. I have learned the hard way not to say 'yes' and then struggle to meet unrealistic deadlines that were impossible from the start. It's very liberating to take control of your business in this way.

There is a reverse side to this booster tip: don't become one of those people who automatically say 'no' to everything. You don't want to be thought cantankerous and difficult to deal with.

Learn to be confident about your own abilities and the value of what you are selling, and if you find yourself in a situation where you are struggling to say 'no' to someone, dig deep to find the resolve you need. The more you do it, the easier it will become.

40 Use simple market research to keep on track

'Market research' is one of those terms that makes people shudder. It sounds complicated and difficult and expensive. It really isn't any of the above; in fact, it's a powerful tool for just about any business. As the name implies, market research simply supplies you with information about your market, or customers. This information can be limitless; it really depends on what you want to know.

Here is an example of how to use market research. A client of mine operated a popular restaurant in a busy tourist town. Although the business was successful, the owners believed that they could increase their existing business by tapping into other potential markets. The first thing we did was carry out a survey of their competitors. We went to every other restaurant in the area to see how my client compared. We surveyed all the hotels in the area to see what their thoughts were on the restaurant, and we introduced a simple questionnaire for customers at the restaurant to fill out at the end of their meal. The information that we collected clearly showed areas that needed to be improved, as well as areas that we could promote and market to increase the number of customers coming to the restaurant. Based on these results we developed a marketing plan, and presto . . . business is now booming.

Market research can be something as simple as keeping a notepad by the phone. When people ring your business, ask them how they found out about you—Yellow Pages, newspaper, word-of-mouth, radio—so that you can tell if your advertising is working.

The key to market research is starting out with the end result in mind. What this means is that you are trying to find answers to specific questions. Don't be afraid of the term 'market research' and look for ways to incorporate it into your business on a day-to-day basis.

The Internet is an excellent tool for collecting market research information. Put a simple questionnaire on your website that encourages people to answer a few questions. Often how we perceive our business is very different from how our customers perceive us. Only market research will give you the right answers. If you are embarrassed about asking questions, pay someone to do it for you.

41 Continually ask your customers if they are happy

Customer satisfaction is the end result of good customer service. So, how do you know if your customers are happy? The simple answer is: you ask them.

I recently had a client who ran a coaching business to help children improve their grades at school. He had about 80 children enrolled, but he wanted to build up the business. One of the areas where I found that he was struggling was a lack of contact with the parents. While he ran an excellent operation and the children achieved great results, he rarely had dealings with the parents except when it came to collecting fees. Most contact was via letters and periodic reports on the children's progress.

I suggested that, instead of sending out letters, he should get on the phone and ring the parents. It would take a few days to call everyone, but he could have a short conversation with each parent to ensure that they were happy with the way things were going and get a commitment from them regarding the future coaching of their children. To his credit he took my advice, rang every parent and the results were fabulous. He achieved a much higher return rate the next semester, he discovered a few problems that could have lost him students which he quickly remedied, and he developed a relationship with his customers—all in all, a very good outcome. Now he rings the parents two or three times a year and his business has continued to grow.

Whenever our company finishes a project, we ask the client to come into the office for a debrief. We sit down and discuss how everything has gone. If there were problems, we try to identify where things went wrong and how it was handled. The good points are discussed, and we ask the client for a testimonial about how they felt our company dealt with their project. This debriefing is extremely valuable for highlighting any problem areas that we may have, and for reinforcing that the customer is happy with the outcome of the project. We also do a follow-up call one month later to ensure that the customer is still happy.

As with market research, if you are uncomfortable asking your customers if they are happy with what you do, get someone else to do it for you. You could send out a simple questionnaire, or employ a marketing company to conduct telephone surveys for you.

An important and mature attitude to market research is essential even if you don't like what you hear. If your customers are telling you that there are problems with your business, you should be very grateful because you may be losing customers. Sometimes when you ask customers for their opinions, you might not like what you hear—but you have to take it on board and be grateful that they have been honest with you.

Customer satisfaction is something that needs to be continually monitored. If it starts to slip, it can reach a point where the damage is very hard to correct. If you are going to boost your business, you need to know what your customers think of your business.

42 Deliver what you promise—if you can't do this, get out of the game

Customer service is all about meeting people's expectations. They will come to your business with a certain expectation of what they will get for their money. If you can't meet this expectation, then maybe you should rethink what you are doing.

An example of this is going on holidays to a wonderful, exotic location. The hotel brochure makes your resort look like paradise. But when you arrive your dreams are shattered when you find yourself trapped in a dump for the next two weeks. Another example is when a product is being advertised on television and the commercial shows lots of warm, friendly staff, standing by for your call to place an order. You give them a call and have to wait for 20 minutes, listening to irritating recorded music. Finally, you get to speak to a bored telesales person who really doesn't care about you or the company—and they are happy to let you know this. Your expectations are shattered once again.

Regardless of what you sell, whether it be a product or a service, to survive and boost your business you need at least to meet, and where possible exceed, your customers' expectations in any way you can. While this may seem an obvious point, it's surprising how many businesses fail to apply this basic business principle. If you are not sure what your customers expect—ask them. Put out a little survey sheet, get on the phone, put in a suggestions box or anything else that you can think of that will let you know exactly what your customers are expecting from you.

43 Be honest and upright in all your dealings

I know that it's a cliché, but honesty is the best policy. At the end of each working day it is important that you believe that everything you have done on that day has been completely honest and scrupulous. If it wasn't, then you are kidding yourself.

There are a lot of business people who lie and cheat—that's a fact of life that is unlikely to change in the near future. However, the successful business people that I deal with are all honest. I believe in karma. I know from my own experience that an honest and scrupulous business generally attracts good people.

If your business is run according to this honesty principle, well done—I'm sure that you are on the path to success. If there are some fuzzy areas in your business, clean them up and adopt an honesty policy today. If you are a complete scam artist, you probably stole this book and one day your karma will catch up with you.

Success is measured in many ways. Running a good business that has strong ethics is a sign of a very successful business.

44 The right and wrong way to handle a complaint

Unfortunately, all businesses have to face the prospect of unhappy customers from time to time. If you are lucky, your customers will tell you when they are not satisfied—giving you the chance to do something about it. If you are unlucky, they will simply fade away, never to return, telling their friends and family that your business should be avoided at all costs.

Sometimes mistakes happen that cause problems and complaints. These mistakes may, or may not, be your fault. The most important aspect of a complaint is to handle it well in an attempt to keep the customer happy enough so that they will continue to use your business and don't become an anti-customer (one who makes it a passion to tell people how bad your organisation is).

The wrong way to handle a complaint is to argue with the customer, to make promises that you can't or won't deliver, to make them feel insignificant or unimportant or, worst of all, to ignore them altogether. I am a letter writer—if I'm not happy with something I write a letter to the manager explaining my side of the story. I am never rude or offensive; I simply write down the details in a simple, logical format, from my point of view. Then I sit back and wait for the answer. Most of the time there is no response at all. I strike these businesses off my list of places to spend my hard-earned money.

From those businesses that are good at handling complaints I normally receive a phone call acknowledging the receipt of my letter and asking me to outline my complaint again. After hearing me out, they tell me exactly how they will follow up the complaint and when they will be in contact with me. They thank me for bringing the problem to their attention and for taking the time to write to them. I am more than happy with this outcome. It isn't my concern if their business succeeds or fails, but I just can't stand to see bad service.

If your business has a clearly defined procedure for handling complaints, you will often find that customers who may once have gone elsewhere are now satisfied and happy. The best outcome is achieved and you reap the benefits.

Now, there is a certain type of customer that we all need to be aware of. They are difficult, unreasonable, incredibly demanding, and often are quite rude. The difficulty is to determine whether a customer is making a reasonable complaint or whether they are an unreasonable customer. If you can honestly say that you have tried to handle a complaint as fairly as possible, yet nothing you do seems to resolve the dilemma, you may have to accept that this particular customer will never be happy and it's time to move on.

Once while working for a cruise company, I encountered a couple who claimed that they had injured themselves on the boat after falling over. The husband claimed that his knee was badly damaged. As a company we did everything we could to help them; we arranged for them to receive medical attention, visited them in their hotel and tried to make sure that everything was OK. A week after they had returned home we received a letter from their lawyer stating that his clients' 'holiday of a lifetime' had been ruined and they were going to sue the company for negligence. The letter stated that his clients had been confined to bed for the duration of their stay and that compensation of $50,000 should be sent immediately, otherwise legal action would commence.

The company was deeply concerned about this claim and started mounting a defence. Being located in a small tourist town, it wasn't long before we heard about a tour guide who was bragging that he had received a $100 tip from a couple of tourists to remove their names from his tour manifest for a safari to the rainforest. Bingo! We soon started collecting more information and before long we had photographs of the 'bedridden' couple on a fishing charter, on a cable car, at a restaurant cabaret and on a high-grade bushwalking tour. We had dates, photos, signatures, the lot. We sent a copy of the photographs to the couple's lawyer and never heard another word.

Of course, this is an extreme case and one that taught me a lot about people. The reality is that 99 per cent of people making a complaint have a justified case that should be handled professionally and the other 1 per cent shouldn't be taken too seriously.

45 Treat your customers with the respect that they deserve

If we don't have customers, we don't have a business. Customers are you and me. I'm not stupid, and I'm sure that you aren't either. So why would we treat our customers as if they are stupid?

We live in modern and exciting times, where there is more choice than ever before. These choices work in our favour as customers, and they make it harder for us as business operators. We have to run a smart business to succeed.

I often see businesses treating their potential customers with little or no respect. They argue with them, try to rip them off, sell them junk, keep them waiting, and generally treat them like second-class citizens. When was the last time you rang or visited a bank that has your money in its vaults, only to be kept on hold for 20 minutes or stuck in a queue for half an hour during the lunchtime rush?

Customers are a powerful group. I believe that customer service will undergo a major renaissance in coming years as we face increasing levels of automation. People will become fed up with talking to machines and will demand better service from other human beings.

Whenever you are dealing with customers, put yourself in their shoes and look long and hard at your business. If you were a customer in your business, would you come back? If the answer is 'yes', that's great—if it's 'no', you might need to rethink your attitude. This booster tip encourages you to treat each and every customer with the respect that they deserve.

46 Learn to recognise when you need a break from your customers

Some days can be really hard. Everyone is driving you crazy—your customers, your staff, your suppliers, the lot. For some reason, everything seems to be going wrong and everything is a drama that requires your attention. The reality is that these days are often no different from any other day; it's more a matter of how you are feeling at the time.

We all need a break from dealing with other people from time to time. I like to go camping with a friend at a remote beach. We spend a week fishing and generally relaxing. My camping buddy works in a high-pressure job as well, so by the time we get in the car and head north we are both ready for some customer-free time. These trips are incredibly therapeutic for me. There are no demands or pressures, and if I don't want to talk I don't have to. There are no social airs and graces; it's simply a time to recharge.

We all have our own recharging methods. If you don't know what yours is, perhaps you need to find out. It took me a number of years to realise that when I am stressed I need a nature fix and time away from people.

If you find that every day is filled with conflict and stress, maybe you need a break from people. It's unlikely that the whole world is out to get you, though at times it may feel like it. Find your de-stresser and use it whenever you need it. If you are finding that you have less patience than normal with your clients, maybe you should try to work behind the scenes for a while. Do those jobs that you have been putting off that need to be done (such as reading a few motivational books, attending a training seminar, doing your tax return or putting together a marketing plan).

Attitude is everything in business. Thriving is often a case of getting to know yourself better.

Notes

....
....
....
....
....
....
....
....
....
....
....
....
....
....
....

Booster Tips Action List

Things to do	Completed
1.	....
2.	....
3.	....
4.	....
5.	....
6.	....
7.	....
8.	....
9.	....
10.	....

7 | Advertising and marketing booster tips

As a marketing consultant I am very passionate about the value of advertising and marketing for any business. I also believe very strongly that good marketing needn't cost a lot of money. It takes a degree of know-how and a simple, clearly defined strategy that is developed according to an individual business's needs, skill levels, budget and the time that the key person can spend actively promoting the business.

This section looks at the basics required to market your business, and at the philosophies behind developing marketing that works and ultimately increases your chances of thriving in a competitive market.

The ideas we'll talk about in this section are:

#47 Develop your own marketing philosophy—what type of business are you?
#48 Do a course or read a marketing book
#49 Take small steps to market your business
#50 Start with looking the part—develop a strong corporate image
#51 Don't be pressured into buying advertising
#52 Market your business to a simple plan
#53 Don't lose touch with your customers
#54 Don't stop marketing because business is booming

#55 If you haven't got the time to market your business, find someone who has

#56 Talk to other people in business

#57 Find a business that you admire

47 Develop your own marketing philosophy—what type of business are you?

What do I mean by having a marketing philosophy? In simple terms, I am asking that you think about your business and the message that you are trying to send to customers. Do you intend to be in business for a long time? Do you want to excel at some particular aspect of business, such as customer service? Do you want to be the biggest or the one with the largest range?

It is important that you have a clear picture in your own mind of exactly what it is you are trying to achieve. For example, Steve's Mediocre Car Repairs probably won't last very long, but Steve's Guaranteed Car Repairs may stand a great chance of being successful and thriving.

Once you have developed your marketing philosophy, you will have a clear picture of the message that you are trying to send to potential customers. I see a lot of businesses that try to be everything to everyone, and I have been guilty of doing this in my own businesses in the past. By having a clear picture of what you are and what you want to be, your chances of attracting new customers are naturally increased.

48 Do a course or read a marketing book

There are three problems that beset most small businesses: a lack of money, a lack of time, and a lack of marketing know-how. The last point is a tough one, because if you haven't had any marketing training it can be difficult to know exactly what you should do.

My first book, *101 Ways to Market Your Business*, has proven to be extremely successful. It contains a lot of simple, practical marketing ideas that can be implemented for very little financial outlay. Judging by the thousands of letters, emails, telephone calls and faxes that I have received, it's clearly a subject that people are passionate about.

There are a number of excellent books that offer step-by-step advice on how to market a business. I have included at the back of this book a list of books that I believe are particularly good. Read as much as you can. For the price of a couple of books, you can find plenty of ideas that will generate more income for your business.

If you can find the time, I really recommend that you do a marketing course. There are hundreds of learning institutes that offer specialist courses ranging from a few hours up to several years in duration.

You will have the edge over your competition if you know more about marketing, and as competition continues to increase we all need as many factors for boosting our business in our favour as possible.

49 Take small steps to market your business

Successful businesses stand out from the crowd because they market and promote themselves well. The aim of all marketing is to attract more customers or to encourage your existing customers to spend more money with your business. By taking a proactive stance to market your business, you can dramatically boost your business.

I often hear people complain that they don't have the money to market and promote their business. I firmly believe that it doesn't necessarily take a lot of money, but it does take commitment and a firm strategy. The task of marketing a business can often become so daunting that it simply doesn't end up being done.

Part of this strategy is to break your marketing into small, manageable components that you can address one by one. All a marketing plan does is identify what you are trying to achieve and how you will achieve it. It outlines the steps that you will take to promote your business and how much you intend to spend on advertising.

If you can break your own marketing down to a few simple steps, it will be easier to implement. I also believe that successful small business marketing is about doing a lot of little things to attract customers. Most of these initiatives cost very little money, but they do take time.

50 Start with looking the part—develop a strong corporate image

I am a firm believer that looking the part is essential to business survival. You might say, 'But what about delivering what you promise, good customer service and value for money? Aren't they more important?' While I believe that these are essential to business success, if you look the part the job becomes much easier.

If you have a good corporate image, you will inspire your customers with confidence in you and your products. If you look a bit rough around the edges, your potential customers may start the relationship with doubts about your business's ability to produce results.

What do I mean by looking the part? The following list will do for starters:

- good, professional stationery (letterheads and business cards);
- clean, professional-looking work space (office, factory or showroom);
- quality signage;
- good company vehicles—not old bombs;
- staff uniforms (where applicable);
- neatly groomed staff;
- well-trained staff (able to answer the phone courteously); and
- a professional website.

Some of the above may not be relevant to you. For example, if you work from home you may not have customers coming to your home, so you probably don't need signage and a showroom. However, don't confuse being a small one-person business with not needing to have a good corporate image.

Often I talk to business owners who are concerned about the cost of professional looking stationery and promotional material. Generally this is a relatively small expense in the overall set-up of a business but it is without a doubt an integral part. From my experience you get what you pay for, so spend a little extra and get the best look and feel stationery you can afford.

Your stationery says a lot about your business on many different levels. The more professional it looks, the more confidence it will instil in your existing and potential customers.

Boosting your business is as much about *looking* the part as it is about *being* the part.

51 Don't be pressured into buying advertising

There are a lot of companies out there that will try to sell you advertising to promote your business. Deciding where to advertise can be difficult and often ends up being decided based on personalities rather than effectiveness—you like one sales representative more than another, so you give them your business.

If advertising doesn't work, why on earth would you do it? I often hear blanket statements such as: 'Television advertising doesn't work', or 'Newspaper advertising doesn't work'. I have seen all types of advertising work very well for individual businesses. The key here is to decide what will work for you.

I believe that anyone trying to sell you advertising needs to qualify your needs. They need to really understand your business, your customers and your expectations. If they don't ask you questions about these issues, how can they possibly sell you a product that works?

All advertising has what is known as a target demographic. This simply defines the kind of people who will see or hear the advertising. Radio stations have different listeners, often at different times; various television shows have specific viewing audiences; and newspapers can have different readers on different days. Within this group there are also times when more people watch, listen or read the various media that are used for advertising. As a result, you pay more to air television commercials when more people are watching television, and you pay more to put a commercial on the radio at drive times, when people tend to be on their way to and from work and are a captive radio audience. These are known as prime times, and virtually all media have them. In newspapers you pay a premium to be in the front of the newspaper, and you pay another premium to be on a right-hand page, which research indicates is a position where more people will see your advertisement.

Advertising sales representatives need to give you this information. Placing advertisements at random in any of the major media is a waste of time and money, in my opinion. Your advertising sales representative needs to really sell you on why you should spend your advertising budget with them. Like any professional advice, I believe that it's fair for you to ask for testimonials from their customers to verify that the advertising works. If a sales representative truly believes in their product, they won't have any hesitation in providing you with a list of names or recommending that you call current advertisers. I also recommend that if you are considering advertising somewhere specific, look for other companies that are advertising there and give them a call to see if it's working for them. Most of the time people will be very open and honest in telling you if their advertising is working or not. I would also suggest that you talk to other business associates and friends to find out where they advertise and to get a second opinion. This only takes a few seconds and it can help you to make the right decision on where to spend your valuable advertising dollars.

There are a lot of excellent media sales representatives around. But remember that their job is to make money for their own company, so they have to sell advertising. Exceptional advertising sales representatives will be looking for ways to make your company money. If the opening line is, 'How can we help your business to attract more customers?' they are talking the right language.

52 Market your business to a simple plan

All businesses should have a marketing plan that they are working to; unfortunately, very few businesses do this. Marketing plans don't have to be long and involved documents; they need only be a few pages long, containing simple pieces of information. By having a plan to work to, your chances of success are dramatically increased because your marketing activity takes on meaning and direction, rather than just reacting as marketing opportunities come across your desk.

A marketing plan should contain the following information:

- a description of how you see your business (from the customer's point of view);
- a list of objectives that you would like to achieve from your marketing activity;
- a description of the type of customers you want to attract (the markets);
- a description of your products or services;
- a list of marketing/advertising that you plan to conduct;
- a budget for how much it will all cost;
- a time frame for implementing the marketing/advertising activity;
- an allocation of responsibilities list—who does what;
- a list of key dates to review results; and
- a list of ways to monitor customer satisfaction.

There are a lot of other things that might be included, but the above items make up the basis of a marketing plan. This document should be referred to often, and I believe that it's a good idea for key staff to be familiar with the contents. It should take no more than a few hours to write a marketing plan along these lines, but the benefits will last all year.

As you start your planning for the next year, review your last marketing plan to see how you went and what you achieved, and what areas you need to put more work into. By putting your marketing plan (or any business plan) in writing, it becomes more permanent and requires following up on. Businesses with marketing plans tend to do more marketing and, as a result, increase their chances of boosting business.

53 Don't lose touch with your customers

By now you will have realised that I am a big advocate of customer service. Happy customers will do more to help your business grow than anything else you can do. When it comes to advertising and marketing, a lot of businesses seem to forget this fact, focusing their attention on placing a few advertisements and waiting for new customers to come along.

There is an old adage that every unhappy customer will tell ten of their friends and associates negative things about your business. If you do the sums, the effect that unhappy customers can have on your business is frightening. Of course, the best way to avoid this terrible anti-advertising is to have happy customers. So, how do you do this? There are a lot of suggestions and recommendations on this subject throughout this book and in my first book, *101 Ways to Market Your Business*. But in a nutshell, you need to stay in touch with your customers.

As your business grows, your attention is often drawn away from the day-to-day activities and often you spend less time with your customers and more time working on behind-the-scenes operational responsibilities. I believe that this is a dangerous time for any business, because it's the time when you can lose touch with what your customers want.

I have seen this happen a number of times. In fact, I think that it has happened to most large organisations. The management are so removed from the actual customers that decisions are made on totally false assumptions of perceived customer satisfaction.

I recently watched a television show that featured the head of the entire British prison system spending a week actually working in a number of prisons throughout England. This was a very senior man who was responsible for an annual budget of hundreds of millions of pounds and employed thousands of people. He wanted to get a feel for the job, so he worked in the prison kitchens, with the warders, in the hospitals and in the prison administrations. Of course, customer satisfaction isn't a prime objective in most prisons, but a real concern was to reduce staff complaints and sick days caused by stress. Following his week spent seeing at first hand how the prison system that he was responsible for actually worked, a number of changes were implemented that solved a lot of problems and resulted in much higher levels of employee satisfaction (and, in some cases, prisoner satisfaction).

The same principle can be applied to any business. I would love to see the head of any major bank in the world have to stand in a queue for an hour during their lunch break because the ATM machine ate their card. Or put the CEO of one of the leading telecommunications companies on hold for 45 minutes and see how they like it.

Don't lose touch with the people that make your business what it is. It's never too late to take the time to talk to your customers and find out their thoughts on how your business is performing.

54 Don't stop marketing because business is booming

Most businesses struggle in the early days; they try lots of different ideas and initiatives and then, bit by bit, business improves and all of a sudden the customers start flocking in. Business is booming.

Once business is booming your bank account is looking healthy, the bank manager remembers your name, and your suppliers have become your new best friends. This is a dangerous time. I have discussed the boom-and-bust cycle earlier in this book; however, there is also the 'we don't need to market our business' syndrome where business is so good that the owners feel that it will always be good.

Unfortunately, you never quite know what is around the corner. If you own a great hamburger shop that is pumping 24 hours a day, would things take a turn for the worse if McDonald's opened up next door? Economies go through cycles of boom and doom: one year your customers may have a lot of money to spend with you, and the next year they may have nothing.

Money comes and goes in cycles and, as a result, so do businesses. I have had a surprising number of clients who had booming businesses for many years and then one day they woke up to find that they were in serious trouble. In almost every one of these instances, they had earlier stopped marketing and promoting their businesses because everything was going so well.

The marketing and advertising you do today will boost your business tomorrow. The better your business is going, the more you should promote it. Many of the people I interviewed for this book said that marketing was essential to the ongoing success of their businesses and that they had learned to promote themselves in both lean times and good times.

55 If you haven't got the time to market your business, find someone who has

Without doubt, time has become one of the greatest commodities of this new century. We are all running around working harder and longer than ever before. It's unlikely that this will change in the near future, so we need to build this time shortage into our daily schedule.

If you find that you don't have enough time to market your business, you may need some professional help in the form of a marketing consultant. There is no shortage of companies that offer these services, and it is up to you to decide exactly what your needs are. You may be better off employing someone to do all of your marketing on a part-time basis.

There are a lot of very talented marketing professionals out there who are looking for businesses to actively promote and market. Their rates are quite reasonable and they can have a real impact on your business. It's also nice to know that if *you* aren't promoting your business, at least someone else is. Of course, there is an expense associated with this, but in the long term your business will benefit.

If you are planning to contract a marketing consultant, take the same approach I outlined for contracting the professional services of a lawyer, financial adviser or accountant. Ask for referrals from other business associates, then interview those consultants that are the most recommended. Ask for a list of their references and contact those people to check that the consultant delivers what they promise.

Discussion of costs and rates is normal prior to the commencement of any work, and I recommend that you get this in writing so that there is no confusion at any stage.

56 Talk to other people in business

One of the best places to get ideas and tips on marketing your business is from other business owners. I am a firm believer in open communication between business owners and operators to share ideas and help each other to grow.

Strategic alliances can be of real benefit. I often catch up with friends who run their own businesses simply to have a chat and to see what they are doing and what is working and what isn't. This is a two-way street, and I offer them information that they may be able to use. If I am reading a newspaper article that is relevant to their industry or their business, I will cut it out and send it to them; they do the same for me. While it's all done very informally, I find that it's very positive and a great way to get a feel for what's happening.

When you run your own business, it's quite easy to become somewhat isolated and to lose touch with what is going on in the real world. This is where the concept of networking began; it was just extended to include doing business directly while networking.

The Internet provides an open window to the world and an opportunity to be exposed to new ideas and sources of inspiration on a daily basis.

57 Find a business that you admire

There are some businesses that just seem to get it right. They have a great image, they have effective advertisements, they have good vehicles and well-dressed staff, their premises look smart and professional, and business appears to be prospering. In most instances, it probably *is* prospering.

I believe that if you model your own business on a business that you admire, your chances of success are enhanced. (It doesn't even need to be a business in the same industry as yours.) In many ways, it's like having a role model or someone to look up to. Whenever you are not sure what you should be doing, have a look at your 'ideal company' and see how they do things. The best thing about this is that once you reach the same level as your role model company, you can actually start to surpass them and become even better at what you do.

Notes

....
....
....
....
....
....
....
....
....
....
....
....
....
....
....

Booster Tips Action List

Things to do	Completed
1.	....
2.	....
3.	....
4.	....
5.	....
6.	....
7.	....
8.	....
9.	....
10.	....

8 | Internet booster tips

The Internet is an exceptional tool for just about every business I encounter. It is there every minute of every day waiting to educate customers, to make sales, to communicate key messages, and so much more. Innovative business owners have realised the true value of the Internet (as have large corporations) and it has become the primary marketing tool for many businesses.

To really boost your business, I suggest revisiting your thoughts towards the Internet and its potential application for you. This section looks at some simple and practical tips that will really help you to take advantage of the World Wide Web and all that it has to offer.

The ideas we'll talk about in this section are:

#58 Be realistic about the Internet
#59 A lousy website makes your business look lousy
#60 Make sure that you market your website
#61 The number one reason that businesses fail on the Internet
#62 Budget for the Internet to be an ongoing expense
#63 Beware of spam

58 Be realistic about the Internet

The Internet is like any other marketing tool—it's bound by financial and creative limitations. If used wisely, the Internet can help your business to grow and become more profitable. The key is understanding how to use the Internet to suit you and your business, and being realistic about what you can achieve financially from your online activity.

We have a number of clients who operate 100 per cent web-based businesses. They have found a market for their products and they have spent many years and a lot of money fine-tuning their businesses to get them to the point where they make money—a lot of money. They will be the first ones to tell you that it's not as easy as most people think. Many business operators have the misconception that if they pay for a website, they will become millionaires overnight. If it was that easy, we would all be doing it.

Consumers aren't stupid, a fact that many people seem to forget when it comes to selling online. People are cautious about giving out credit card details, they are suspicious that what is promoted on a website will prove to be a cheap copy when it arrives, and they don't like to wait weeks for delivery. For this reason, the most successful websites sell familiar products that consumers feel comfortable buying online, such as books and CDs. Other successful online products are niche products that have a very particular market. These businesses are successful because their customers find it hard to buy their products elsewhere.

The Internet has many uses apart from selling products. For instance, it can be used to promote your business 24 hours a day. We recently developed a website for an organic dairy farm. They were selling farm-fresh products throughout the region and, like any business, they had limited resources. The website served many purposes for their small operation:

- It provided background information about the business and the types of products they sold.

- It showed pictures of the farm (which consumers love to see).
- It provided recipes and recommendations for ways to use their extensive range of products.
- It told consumers where they could buy the products.
- It provided space for people to add their comments about the product.
- It provided information about a home delivery service that was available.
- It allowed people living in the area to order the products directly from the farm.

All in all, the website served as an order taker, marketing company, public relations consultant and information resource, all operating 24 hours a day, seven days a week. Although the business had limited resources, the website made it appear large and professional while still maintaining its cottage appeal.

The Internet is here to stay, so anyone in business needs to come to grips with how to incorporate it into the day-to-day processes of their business and use it to its full potential.

I recently undertook a project for a small company that had been struggling financially for some years. They set up a good website to sell their products and increased their annual turnover by $600,000, which lifted them out of the financial graveyard.

The most important point to make about the Internet is that you need to have a plan or a strategy in place so that you know what you are trying to achieve. Your Internet plan needs to have the following five key components:

1. A clear understanding of what you are trying to achieve. Do you want to sell products, pass on information, promote your business, attract new customers, or offer additional services to existing customers?
2. A budget. How much money can you commit each year to make your site do all of the things that you want it to do?

Set aside a realistic amount that you can afford and go from there.

3. Some innovation. Look at other sites and try to find things that other businesses are doing that you could adapt and use on your site to make it more innovative and professional.

4. Check out your competitors' websites to identify the good, the bad and the ugly things about their sites that you can either improve on or avoid.

5. Ask your customers to give you feedback about your site, and listen to their suggestions and comments.

Developing an Internet strategy needn't be a long or involved process, but having one will increase your chances of boosting business. Sit down and write down all the things you would like to achieve with your website and then find someone to make it happen. Just putting a few product pictures on a website seldom works. Instead, put customer testimonials on your site and use other people to tell the world how great you are. Include a full list of products and services, plenty of photographs (including photos of you and your staff to make it personal). Reduce text to a minimum, and make the site colourful and impressive. Research indicates that you have about six seconds to catch someone's attention when they visit your website if they are just browsing, so make sure that your home page loads quickly and looks sensational.

59 A lousy website makes your business look lousy

Website technology is changing rapidly. I recently visited a website that I developed several years ago and which hadn't been updated much in that time. It looked like it had been designed a hundred years ago. Websites need to look impressive from the start and to be updated regularly.

The cost to develop a good website is becoming cheaper every day. I recommend that you spend as much as you can comfortably afford. If you can't afford anything just yet, don't panic—work towards developing one as your cash flow suits.

If you are planning to develop a website in stages, make sure that you let your web developer know as it can save you a lot of money in the future if the site is built with room for expansion.

Whenever I am developing an Internet site for a client I spend some time surfing the Net and looking at what their competitors around the world are doing. Then I check out a multitude of unrelated sites, looking for novel ideas. If I find a site that I like the look of, I bookmark it and show it to the web designer as an example of what we are looking for.

For many potential customers, your website will be their first point of contact with your business and they will make a decision about whether or not they would like to take the next step based on what they see there. I believe that a good website has a number of key components:

- It loads quickly. If your site takes a while to load, have the designer put something on the screen to interest the viewer and keep their attention.
- Use of simple colours. But remember that different computers see colours differently. What looks great on the designer's computer may look lousy on your customers' screens.
- Includes customer testimonials.
- Minimal text, but has places on the site where more information can be found.

- Avoids using plug-ins that people have to download. Remember that people want to go to your site to determine if they want to buy what you are selling. Make it easy for them.
- Uses pictures of actual people. I am surprised that the majority of websites are so anonymous. To me it's the perfect opportunity to introduce you and your team to potential customers and it puts a human face on your business, which encourages people to buy.
- Not slowed down by bells, whistles, flashing lights and moving pictures. They are all pretty to watch, but often all they do is slow down the site and create barriers to customers finding out about your products.
- Has banner advertisements that take customers to other areas of the site, *not* away from the business. Any advertising on the site should be used to promote your business.

These tips should help you to build a website that works and encourages people to find out more about your business.

60 Make sure that you market your website

If you are going to have a website, you need to market and promote it. Waiting for people who are surfing the Net to find it is definitely hit-or-miss, and a lack of marketing is the main reason why websites fail.

There are many different terms used to measure the traffic flow or number of people who visit a website and I find the term 'unique visitors' the most appropriate. This means that if the same person visits a website 50 times in a month (from the same computer) they are still only measured as one unique visitor. Attracting as many unique visitors as possible to a site is quite a science and there are many companies that offer this as a specialised service. They have the technical know-how to achieve this result and it really is an integral part of any website strategy or online plan.

You can play an active role in marketing your own website by making certain that your web address is printed on every single piece of promotional material your company produces—cars, uniforms, stationery, signs, invoices, packaging, the products themselves, and anything else you can think of.

It doesn't take a lot of time or cost a lot of money to link your site to other sites and this is an excellent way to increase traffic flow to your website. I suggest that you be selective about the sites that you choose to link to and from, otherwise your credibility can be affected.

Whenever you advertise your business, you should include your web address. This reinforces the importance of having a good domain (website) name that is easy to remember. If you don't market your website, no one will visit it. The best website with no visitors is about as useful as a great book that no one reads.

61 The number one reason that businesses fail on the Internet

Everyone is trying to sell something on the Internet but, not surprisingly, very few businesses are successful at online selling. My successful Internet clients all agree that the number one reason why Internet selling fails is because the business takes too long to respond to an enquiry.

The Internet is the ultimate instantaneous device. At any time of the day or night you can find out about virtually anything in the world. While many businesses can offer online and real time sale of products or services, many still require more detailed email correspondence; for example, to gather additional information before a price can be submitted. Businesses that succeed online are quick to respond (even allowing for time differences that should definitely be within 24 hours).

Those companies that answer their email enquiries very quickly will sell more products than those that take a long time to respond. I am constantly surprised by how slow many businesses are in processing emails and responding to requests for prices or other information. I wanted to do a diving trip with great white sharks in South Australia recently. I emailed five companies that offered this service and not one responded to my request. I emailed six companies in South Africa that also offer the same service and all six responded—albeit several took over a week to get back to me, but at that stage any response was a good one.

Once again, the whole idea of having a website is to encourage people to do business with you. If you are lucky enough to have them interested in buying something from you, respond to their emails as soon as possible. This shows that you value their business, and that you are organised and efficient and therefore credible. It's easy enough these days to have an automatic response which at least acknowledges that you have received their email and you will be in touch shortly.

This same principle applies to any form of contact from prospective customers—respond quickly and you will have a far greater chance of getting their business. I remember reading a fascinating article once which said that the number one reason for lost sales and lost customers was poor communication. More specifically, it was a lack of follow-up. We have all experienced the old 'I'll call you straight back' and 'You'll have the price on your desk in the morning' lines. To really boost your business, follow up quickly and efficiently—not just on the Internet, but with all communications—and your chances of thriving will increase significantly.

62 Budget for the Internet to be an ongoing expense

Step one with the Internet is to make a plan and decide exactly what you want to achieve. Step two is to develop your site, and step three is to keep updating it. You will need to budget for the Internet as an ongoing cost. It isn't a simple one-off cost that you pay and then forget about.

How much you need to spend each year is up to you and will depend on the size and complexity of your site. There is nothing worse than looking at a website that isn't up-to-date and where the news flash on the bottom of the home page refers to an event that happened some time ago.

If you can't afford to update your website on a regular basis, be careful about putting any information online that will quickly become dated. I often see signs saying when the website I am looking at was last updated. This is great if it was yesterday, but the site's credibility suffers if it was 12 months ago.

As with all expenses, budget what you can afford and allow for the upgrading of your website on a regular basis.

63 Beware of spam

If I get one more email marked 'Extremely important', only to open it and find that it's from someone I have never heard of trying to sell me something I don't want, I will scream. Spam is the electronic version of junk mail. If you have an email account, you will get spam. I have two major gripes with spam. The first is when companies send me large spam files that take a long time to download, and the second is those companies that send me junk every other day. Another concern with spam is the spread of viruses. I am very cautious about this issue and I now delete any mail that I am in the slightest bit suspicious about.

I predict that people will really start to get fed up with spam as time goes on and the amount increases. We are now faced with receiving the same unsolicited advertising on our mobile phones. The main reason for the increasing amount of spam is that it is by far the cheapest and easiest way to reach a lot of people, with little more than the press of a few buttons.

Email is a great way to promote your business, but use it in a sensible and considerate manner. Keep any correspondence short and to the point, and only retain the essential parts of any emails you are responding to. If your company is guilty of sending out lots of spam mail, you may be doing your reputation more harm than good. There are a number of companies that I will never deal with simply because they keep bombarding me with junk.

My booster tip is to use email wisely. Don't upset potential customers by bombarding them with hundreds of unsolicited emails every other day. Use it as a tool that can sell your business, but use it in a responsible manner.

Notes

....
....
....
....
....
....
....
....
....
....
....
....
....
....
....
....

Booster Tips Action List

Things to do	Completed
1.	....
2.	....
3.	....
4.	....
5.	....
6.	....
7.	....
8.	....
9.	....
10.	....

9 | Insurance booster tips

Insurance is very important in this age of litigation. It is also important for peace of mind in myriad other areas—for example, what happens to your business if you fall ill and can't work for six months? There are many types of insurance products available and it can be daunting to decide what kind of insurance you should have. A key principle in this section is being informed about insurance at all levels, from choosing the right company or insurance broker to minimising your risks and reading the fine print.

The ideas we'll talk about in this section are:

#64 What type of insurance should you have?
#65 How much insurance should you have?
#66 Always read the fine print
#67 Make sure that you meet your requirements as per the policy schedule
#68 Using an insurance broker
#69 Don't just sign the renewal policy—always compare products and prices
#70 Prevention is better than cure

64 What type of insurance should you have?

I have insurance for just about everything. I'm sure that some-where among my policies there is even a 'disruption to business caused by alien invasion' policy. One of the best insurance policies that I have is income protection. This means that if I can't work for health reasons, I receive a monthly payment up until age 65. This is very reassuring, because you never know what could happen. If I was debilitated to the point of not being able to work, I doubt very much that I could meet my monthly commitments on a government sickness benefit. This policy is expensive (about $2000 per annum), but it certainly helps me to sleep at night.

There are lots of different policies that cover everything from the everyday liabilities, to burglary, fire and theft, personal injury, and so on. However, the insurance industry is dynamic and constantly evolving, resulting in new policies being developed all the time that may suit your business and personal requirements perfectly.

Business survivalists are big believers in insurance. Budget for insurance to cover as many possibilities as you can, and remember to stay abreast of changes to the insurance products available.

65 How much insurance should you have?

The simple answer to this is: as much as you can afford, and in most cases more. Insurance is one of those expenses that is often seen as a luxury because it doesn't actually bring any money into the business on a day-to-day basis. Unfortunately, the truth is that without insurance you have very little security, and the small amount of money you save on premiums can become insignificant when your business and your income are adversely affected.

An important point to remember with insurance is that your needs change constantly. As your business grows you may have more plant and equipment to protect, more customers on your premises which could increase your chances of someone being injured, greater personal wealth, and often debt needing higher levels of cover to ensure that if you do have an untimely death your family and business partners won't be left holding the bill.

Talk to your legal adviser to ensure that you are legally covered insurance-wise and that you have adequate personal insurance. I look at it from the point of view that, if I died tomorrow, would my family have enough money for a degree of financial security (but not enough to make them encourage me to take up crocodile wrestling for a living)?

No one likes to arrive at work to find that the premises have been burgled, but it's much easier to take when you know that you are fully covered. So, take out as much insurance as you can afford.

66 **Always read the fine print**

Like any legally binding contract, you really do need to be aware of the fine print on insurance policies. I live in an area that is prone to flooding and cyclones, which I guess is an insurance nightmare. My policies are all worded very technically about the situations where I am covered and where I am not. Basically, if damage is caused by water coming in from the roof, I am covered; however, if damage is caused by water rising up from a flood, I am not covered. There are a number of grey areas, such as storm surges and damage caused by a cyclone battering the roof. The bottom line is that you really need to know exactly what you are covered for.

I make up a list of questions when taking out any new insurance policy. I ask my insurance broker (see Booster Tip #68) to show me where my questions are answered on the policy form, and if I'm not sure about anything I call my lawyer. I know that this adds to the expense, but at least I know exactly where I stand. There is nothing worse than standing beside a destroyed building with the insurance assessor pointing to clause 455 which basically means you are not covered in this instance. That sinking feeling lasts for a long time.

We all receive a lot of junk mail about insurance policies for this and that. If you die tomorrow, your family will get $1 million and it will only cost you $10 a month, and so on. If you check the fine print there are often lots of conditions, and sometimes one policy can override other policies, so you may end up paying for other policies which, if you made a claim, would be cancelled because of your new policy.

Remember that, at the end of the day, insurance companies don't want to pay you. They are taking a risk that the things you are insuring against won't happen. If they do happen, they will be looking for a way (a loophole) to get out of sending you a cheque. I'm not saying that insurance companies are unethical; I'm saying that they are tough. As a consumer, you need to be aware of exactly what you have signed and are paying for—ignorance is not an excuse.

If you have any doubts at all regarding your insurance, get some professional advice to make absolutely certain that you are covered.

67 Make sure that you meet your requirements as per the policy schedule

This really means that you need to qualify for cover, and stay qualified. Insurance policies are very detailed on what you need to advise the insurer about. If your situation changes and you don't advise the insurance company, you may void your policy.

An example of this could be that you are required to have a particular type of alarm to protect your business from burglary or fire. In the normal course of business you may decide to buy a new alarm which is technically better, but it may not meet your insurer's requirements. If your premises are then burgled or destroyed by fire, this may provide the insurance company with an 'out' as you haven't held up your end of the bargain and they may get out of paying you.

Another important point to remember, especially with the less well-known types of insurance, is that you will be required to answer a lot of questions and you need to answer them accurately. A simple mistake or a lie can void the policy when it comes time to make a claim, so it just isn't worth it. Fill in all the details as honestly and accurately as possible.

68 Using an insurance broker

Insurance is a complicated and involved industry with lots of choices and a great deal of technical wording. Using an insurance broker to help you through the process can be very beneficial.

To find a good insurance broker, you need to follow the same steps as when finding any professional adviser. Ask friends and other business associates for a recommendation, discuss your needs with the potential broker or brokers, and ask them for some client testimonials and their contact details so that you can establish for yourself that the individual or company you are thinking of dealing with is as good as they say they are.

If they won't give you this information, don't deal with them. Insurance is an important part of your business—your future could depend on it. You need practical advice, from a knowledgeable source who can prove to you that they know what they are doing.

A question that is not often asked is which company you will ultimately be insured by. Often by the time you get the policy in the mail, the name at the top is different from the name you thought would appear there. In light of recent insurance company failures throughout the world, you may prefer to deal with companies that are secure. Your insurance broker should be able to give you advice in this area, although they are not privy to the internal workings of insurance organisations so they cannot be 100 per cent certain of the liquidity of any particular company.

Likewise, you need to be honest with your insurance broker. If you have made claims in the past, tell them. It will save everyone a lot of time and will eliminate the risk of your having a claim rejected because you provided false information.

A point that I have made throughout this book is that businesses that prosper look for professionals to give them advice. I recommend using an insurance broker, because they will sell you products that suit your business. Going directly to an insurance company means that they can only sell you the products that they offer. Insurance is a very important part of any business. If you haven't been sold a good policy, your business may not survive when it comes time to make a claim. Like any professional advisers, there are good insurance brokers and some that are not so good. Follow the steps outlined in this book to find any professional adviser and you will increase your chances of finding a good one.

69 Don't just sign the renewal policy—always compare products and prices

Most insurance companies send annual renewal notices through the mail. The easiest thing to do is simply sign it, add a cheque or credit card details, and send it back. From my experience, this isn't necessarily the best thing to do.

Throughout the year there may have been changes to your policy that you are not really aware of. You may be breaching your requirements and not even know about it and, odds on, you won't know about it until you make a claim.

Apart from the policy itself changing there may be new products available that are more suited to your needs and requirements. It really does pay to take the time to find out if there are any changes to the policy and whether there are other products in the marketplace that will better suit your needs. If you use a broker, they should look after this for you. However, you should keep in mind that if you sign the form, you are responsible. Buyer beware.

The basic booster tip regarding all insurance is to shop around, meet your obligations, stay aware of any changes and, if you feel it is appropriate, get professional advice.

70 Prevention is better than cure

This old cliché is still particularly relevant in the area of insurance. Look for ways to protect yourself while minimising your insurance costs wherever possible. Good work practices and a safe working environment are preferable to a legal case involving an injured person suing you and your insurance company.

The more risks you can reduce or eliminate, the better off you will be. I often think that people can become complacent once they sign an insurance policy, almost as if the cover they get means they no longer have to try and do the right thing. Talk to your insurance company or broker about ways in which you can reduce your risks and, as a result, your insurance premiums. Often there are some simple security measures that can be implemented that will result in lower costs; it's just a matter of finding out what they are.

Insurance is a back-up for those times when bad things happen. It's preferable, however, to take steps to minimise the risk of those things happening.

Notes

....
....
....
....
....
....
....
....
....
....
....
....
....
....
....

Booster Tips Action List

Things to do	Completed
1.	....
2.	....
3.	....
4.	....
5.	....
6.	....
7.	....
8.	....
9.	....
10.	....

10 | Legal booster tips

At some stage in your business career you will need professional legal advice. This section identifies how to find a good lawyer and use their services in a cost-effective manner. It looks at ways to reduce your own legal risks and considers some areas where you need to be particularly careful.

Our dependence on professional legal advice will likely continue to increase. From my own experience, good legal advice will more than pay for itself over time.

The ideas we'll talk about in this section are:

#71 When to use a lawyer
#72 Choosing a lawyer
#73 Keeping legal costs down
#74 Make sure that everything is up-front
#75 Get a second opinion
#76 Even lawyers make mistakes—take control and ask questions
#77 The real cost of taking someone to court—is it worth it?
#78 Make sure that everything is in writing

71 When to use a lawyer

One reason that we all use lawyers is to protect ourselves from future legal problems. Most business operators use lawyers to review formal documents such as leases, wills and last testaments, and contracts between business stakeholders. The bottom line is that it's far more sensible to spend money on hiring a lawyer to protect yourself than to wait for someone to sue you, resulting in the loss of everything you own.

Any formal agreement should be reviewed by your lawyer. When you are signing a lease on a new premises, your lawyer should review it to ensure that all the details are correct and that you are being treated fairly. If your business is a partnership, your solicitor should be involved in drawing up the partnership agreement, just as they should be if your partnership is being dissolved. In reality, any situation that involves some form of financial risk should have input from your solicitor.

There are many stories of businesses that have gone broke because they were left legally unprotected by trying to save a few dollars in legal fees. This booster tip is all about being pre-pared for the worst. Try to develop a good rapport with your lawyer, to the point where you can ring them to ask their advice without necessarily being charged.

I strongly advocate trying to resolve any conflicts as quickly as possible. The longer a case drags on, the more money it will cost and the more time you will have to devote to non-productive issues rather than the business itself.

72 Choosing a lawyer

Before choosing a lawyer, it's important to decide exactly what legal services you require. If you have a complex business involving a lot of contracts, written agreements and information going out to clients, your needs may be more involved than a business that simply sells products (like a restaurant or shop). This determines what kind of lawyer you may require. For example, as a writer and marketing consultant I need a lawyer who understands copyright law.

I have discussed the process of choosing a professional adviser a number of times in this book, and I recommend that you follow the same process when deciding on which lawyer will best suit your needs. Ask your business associates for referrals. Are they happy with the lawyer that they have been using? Who would they suggest you avoid using, based on bad past experiences?

Once you have a few names, arrange a preliminary interview with each firm (which should be free) to explain your legal requirements and to see if they can meet your needs at a reasonable cost. Ask questions about the firm's current clients, the type of work they specialise in and their charges, and request some testimonials from clients who can verify their abilities and professionalism. An impressive office doesn't mean that a particular law firm is good at what they do—it just means they have a good interior designer.

Discussing costs up-front is a very normal business practice; if you don't ask how much their advice will cost you, you may be in for a nasty surprise.

73 Keeping legal costs down

Lawyers have a reputation for being expensive, and from my experience this is generally true. (I once received a bill from a law firm that was 300 pages long and totalled over $30,000. On top of this, I had to pay $4000 to have another firm review the bill, looking for mistakes such as charges levied for letters that were never written, faxes that weren't sent and meetings that didn't take place.)

There are a number of ways to keep costs down when using a lawyer, and the best way is to do as much as possible of the legwork yourself. (The same goes for accountants. The more organised your records are, the less your accountant will charge to prepare your records.) When dealing with your lawyer, get into the habit of asking them how to keep the costs down. Always ask for options, and really get the message across that you want to save money where possible.

Some legal firms are willing to take a case on speculation, where they get paid only if and when you win a particular action. This can be a good option if you don't have a lot of money up-front; however, the cut that they take is normally very high (30–40 per cent). The choice is up to you and, of course, the individual firm's policy.

A theme that I have emphasised in this book is the development of relationships with key people in your business life. These key people can include your lawyer, accountant, bank manager, landlord and marketing consultant. If you have a good relationship with your lawyer, they may be a bit kinder when it comes to billing. (I know that as a marketing consultant I tend to be pretty soft when billing clients that I like.)

Look for ways to keep your legal costs as low as possible, but don't avoid using a lawyer because of fear of the expense. Businesses that thrive have good legal advice.

74 Make sure that everything is up-front

If you are going to use a lawyer, there is no point in trying to hide information from them. If you have done something wrong or made a mistake, it really is in your best interest to tell your lawyer everything. Your lawyer is on your side and there to protect you or work towards the best outcome. Therefore, the fewer surprises that they encounter, the better.

When I first started using lawyers a long time ago, I always felt a little embarrassed. My letters were poorly filed, I didn't keep all of my records, and I often didn't tell the whole story because I thought the lawyer would think less of me. The thing you need to remember is that lawyers see lots of people with myriad problems every day, so the odds are that your particular problem isn't unique. Don't be embarrassed, lay everything on the line and be completely honest with your lawyer.

In regard to costs, you are perfectly entitled, before proceeding with legal action of any sort, to ask for a written quote up-front outlining what costs you can expect and when you will have to pay them.

It's also well worth asking what will happen if you lose your case. Will you be liable for the other party's costs as well as your own? Be 100 per cent clear in your mind as to exactly what costs you are liable for now, and what costs you could be liable for if things don't go as planned.

I also like to have some idea from my lawyer of how long an action may take or when certain steps will be completed. Some of these things may be out of the lawyer's hands, particularly things like setting dates for court appearances, but they should have a fairly good idea.

75 Get a second opinion

There can only be one winner in a law suit, so if you are pursuing legal action against another person or company, be prepared for the fact that you may be the loser. What will losing mean to you financially, professionally, emotionally, and so on?

Lawyers sometimes get it wrong. I strongly recommend that, in cases where the outcome is important, you get a second opinion. Your lawyer may think you have an excellent chance of winning, but a second opinion may reveal that your chances of winning aren't as good as you first thought. Just as you should feel comfortable about getting a second opinion on medical matters, you should feel comfortable about getting a second opinion on legal matters.

Several years ago I was thinking about taking legal action against a company over an injury that I suffered due to their negligence. I saw five lawyers of whom four said that it would be a waste of time and not to bother. They all said that it would take years, cost a lot of money, and the outcome was likely to go against me. In hindsight, I don't think they wanted to take on the case. The fifth law firm was great. They were a big firm, with a good background in my type of case. They encouraged me to pursue the matter, which was settled in my favour five years later for $150,000. I wouldn't say it was easy, but if I had taken the advice of the other lawyers I would have dropped the case.

You should weigh up the situation for yourself and assess a number of opinions before going ahead. Don't be afraid to ask for a second opinion in any professional dealing.

76 Even lawyers make mistakes—take control and ask questions

I have had some shocking experiences with legal firms. Once my lawyer forgot to turn up to court and we subsequently lost the case. One firm worked on a case of mine for six years but did little in that time except add a few notes to my file. And one firm took so long to proceed with an action that the company I was suing for non-payment of a bill went broke and I not only lost a large amount of money but had to pay hefty legal fees.

I have spoken to many other business people who have had very similar experiences and they all agree that there isn't a lot you can do about it. Of course, you could sue your solicitor, which will be difficult, costly and time-consuming. The other option is to be a squeaky wheel—ask lots of questions and make certain that you are absolutely up-to-date and informed at every step of your legal proceeding. If you don't understand how something works, keep asking questions until you are very clear about it. Take notes, and ask for copies of all correspondence to be sent to you (which they should do anyway).

This booster tip is all about taking control of your legal matters. If in doubt, ask, and make certain that you know exactly what is happening, why it is happening and when it is happening.

77 The real cost of taking someone to court—is it worth it?

If you are faced with the real possibility of taking someone to court, it's important to spend some time assessing whether or not it's actually worth it. Court proceedings take a long time, cost a lot of money and can be very stressful. I'm not suggesting that you should simply write off old accounts or walk away from disputes. I *am* saying that you need to weigh up the pros and cons and then make an informed decision.

In my business I have had to chase people for money many times. We tend to follow this procedure:

1. Hire someone to call all of our clients who have overdue accounts. This generally results in some of the overdue money being paid and it isn't threatening. It's more along the lines of: 'Hey, your account is dragging on a bit and we would appreciate it if you could sort it out.'
2. Repeat the above step a few weeks later and ask for a commitment to a specific date for payment or make arrangements for a payment plan.
3. Follow up on the above. If some clients still won't commit to pay, we threaten legal action.
4. Start legal action against those clients who still refuse to pay. Sometimes we get our money, but most of the time we don't.

The same principle applies to other types of legal disputes: the only real winners are the lawyers. Of course, there are times when you have to fight for what you believe in, and the law is there to protect the innocent party. However, many people have lost a lot of money by embarking on a court case on a matter of principle.

The bottom line is that legal action should be avoided where possible. An alternative is to use a mediator to try and resolve a dispute. Both parties agree to be bound by the decision of the mediator whose main role is to try and resolve the conflict in the fairest possible way to both parties.

In many countries the legal system now makes mediation a standard step on the journey to court in an attempt to free up court facilities and the judges' time formerly tied up with petty and small claims.

78 Make sure that everything is in writing

The day of the handshake agreement has, sadly, come to an end. If you find that a lot of your business agreements are only verbal and there is nothing in writing, you may need to review the way that you do business.

I have worked very hard at developing systems that protect us and the companies that we deal with. If it's in writing and both parties have a copy, there really is no room for argument at a later date. Like a lot of relationships, everything may be fine in the early stages, but if it sours you need to be protected by paperwork.

All agreements with suppliers, staff, customers, lawyers, and so on, need to be confirmed in writing. Another excellent habit to get into is to write summaries of meetings and discussions in your diary. If there is a dispute somewhere down the line, your diary can be submitted as evidence. I had to give evidence in a legal matter several years ago and I had to present my diary outlining meetings on specific dates, what was discussed and any follow-up.

The main point of this booster tip is to encourage you to write down any information that could be important at a later date. File it where you'll know where to find it if you need it. Save your old diaries. I have diaries going back 12 years. I now use my diary to record anything that could later be disputed.

Notes

....
....
....
....
....
....
....
....
....
....
....
....
....
....
....
....

Booster Tips Action List

	Things to do	Completed
1.	....	....
2.	....	....
3.	....	....
4.	....	....
5.	....	....
6.	....	....
7.	....	....
8.	....	....
9.	....	....
10.	....	....

11 | Personal booster tips

Apart from all the day-to-day business activities that we have to deal with, there are many personal pitfalls that we can encounter in business. Many of these can affect the overall success of our business, and thus they need to be allowed for if we are to boost our business.

This section highlights those aspects of running a business that can affect you on a personal level. They include stress and burnout, managing your home life as well as your business, and simple forms of development that will be good both for you and your business.

The ideas we'll talk about in this section are:

#79 Start your business feeling refreshed and healthy
#80 Don't give up your hobbies when you start your business
#81 Try to separate work from home
#82 Maintaining your enthusiasm
#83 Learn to laugh and lighten up
#84 Learn to handle stress
#85 Listen to your instincts—they are normally right
#86 Take regular holidays, even though there is never a good time
#87 Develop your negotiating skills
#88 Be supportive of the community where you make your living
#89 Use photographs to record your progress

#90 Know when to call it a day
#91 Break the habit of doing things the way they've always been done
#92 Don't be afraid to make changes (name, location, etc.)
#93 Keep copies of important documents

79 Start your business feeling refreshed and healthy

I am a firm believer in starting any new business or project feeling refreshed and healthy. To survive and build strong foundations, you will need a clear mind and a body with enough energy to do what you ask of it.

The early stages of a new business can be very exciting. There is always a lot to do, and your attention needs to be focused on many different areas, often calling on skills and expertise outside of your normal day-to-day experience. It's also a time that can be very challenging and, in many ways, difficult, especially if you start to have negative thoughts, particularly about all the money you may be spending to set up your business.

Because of this you really need to be feeling good, both mentally and physically. If you start out tired and run-down it's likely that you will only get worse as time goes on. You need to be sharp and focused, with a clear plan of attack. Being good at what you do is important when it comes to setting up a successful business, but having stamina and a clear mind is equally as important.

I see a lot of people running small businesses who are burned-out shells, simply going through the motions, with no real enthusiasm or zest for life. From my experience, customers don't like to deal with people like this because they come across as being negative.

If you are finishing your old job on Friday and starting your own business on Monday, you may be in for trouble. Take a break, do some exercise and eat well. Build yourself up so that when you start your business you are bulletproof and filled with enthusiasm for the project you are about to undertake.

80 Don't give up your hobbies when you start your business

As something of a workaholic, I can attest to the fact that owning and operating your own business can become all-consuming. You will have a lot of demands placed on you from every direction. Combine this with enthusiasm and passion for what you are doing, and suddenly your life will be filled with just one thing—your business. I have used every excuse known to mankind when trying to justify why I have to spend yet another weekend in the office and not with my family or friends. After a while the phone stops ringing and often relationships break down.

Running a successful business is, without a doubt, one of life's greatest challenges. There are many benefits and many pitfalls, and maintaining a balance between them is essential to long-term success. Many of my business friends complain that they no longer have the time to do the things they enjoy because they are always working. If you are in this situation, you really need to ask yourself: is it all worth it?

I strongly recommend that you maintain interests outside of your business. I wrote up a list of the things I love to do when I have free time. Next to each of the items I noted when I did it last. The results were a little scary and they motivated me to spend more time doing the things that I love, that are purely recreational. My list included things like fishing, playing squash, camping, bushwalking, writing, reading, having dinner with friends and cooking.

The biggest bonus from doing the things you love is that you go back to work feeling bright and fresh, and I honestly believe that you are much more productive. If nothing else, you will be a much nicer person to be around. I also get some of my best business ideas while sitting in a boat waiting for a fish to tug on the end of my line.

My booster tip here is that any business can become all-consuming. It's up to you to ensure that it doesn't.

81 Try to separate work from home

This booster tip is most applicable to two types of business people: those who run their business from home, and those who work with their partner. I have been in both situations on several occasions and have no doubt that keeping work and home separate is essential not only to your sanity but also to your overall success.

Working from home can be great. There are a lot of books written on the subject filled with practical advice and ideas on how to make it work. The main problems that I have experienced with working from home are:

- It's too easy to work all the time.
- Family and friends don't take your work seriously.
- There are a lot of distractions.
- Some people don't take home-run businesses seriously.

Of course, there are also a lot of benefits! The best booster tip that I can recommend for home-based businesses is to separate work and home. One way of doing this is to have some sort of physical barrier, such as a sign on a door, a separate entrance, or anything that makes you feel that you are entering your work space. Family and friends also need to understand that this is your work space, not a social room, and that, just as if you were working in an office or a shop, you need to get work done when you are there.

If you are working with your spouse or partner there are a lot of potential problems. Discussing your company's profit and loss statement does *not* qualify as foreplay in the romantic arena! Your enthusiasm and excitement about running your own business can often take over your life, and so it is critical that you set some ground rules. Some rules that I have used include:

- No talking about work after 7 p.m.
- Spend time apart outside of the business.

- Clearly define roles within the business.
- Keep time for you as a couple, not as business partners.
- Leave personal problems at home and business problems at work.

If you mention that you work with your partner, many people will gasp and ask how you both manage it. Without a doubt it is hard, but if you have a plan and stick to it I believe that you can make it work.

The most important booster tip for couples working together is to separate work from home.

82 Maintaining your enthusiasm

Maintaining enthusiasm can be tough for all of us, particularly on those days when it just doesn't seem to be happening and what *can* go wrong *does* go wrong, and you end up asking yourself what on earth you are doing. Don't worry, we all have those days, and we all have a little trouble staying positive at times. I have four techniques that I use:

- I read something motivational about someone who really had things to complain about but didn't.
- I surround myself with positive people who are happy to share their positive energy.
- I pull out those jobs that I really enjoy doing and just work on those for the day.
- I goof off—I go and see a movie, have lunch with friends, buy a new shirt, or do something completely unrelated to what is driving me crazy. It's not very responsible, but it sure makes me feel better.

I am very lucky, as I believe that I was born with more than my fair share of optimism. But while it comes naturally, it's tested often. I find that some people manage to inspire me to keep going when I really don't feel like it. We are all only human, we will have good days and bad days, but as long as the good outweigh the bad we really can't be doing too badly.

I am also a firm believer in maintaining your health to maintain your enthusiasm. You don't have to be a health fanatic—I certainly am not—but I know that if I'm feeling tired and run-down, and my enthusiasm is waning, then eating well and going for a few long walks can really help. The best piece of advice I can offer is not to be too hard on yourself. If you are having trouble maintaining your enthusiasm, the odds are that it's only temporary, so don't worry.

83 Learn to laugh and lighten up

We all take ourselves too seriously from time to time. There really isn't that much to be serious about, but in our quest to be successful we can put ourselves under enormous pressure. One of the biggest bonuses of running your own business is the fact that you are the boss and the decisions you make ultimately decide your future. It sounds pretty heavy, but in reality you can only do your best.

We could all benefit from lightening up and taking things a bit easier from time to time. I am often amazed by people who seem to be doing a million things at once—juggling a family, their own business, bills, staff, customers, and so on—yet who can still find the time to stop and have a laugh, often at their own expense.

I had one client who encouraged his staff to take it in turns finding a joke for the day. There were five staff and they all had a day to come up with a joke. My client said that it lightened up the mood in the workplace, as laughter and humour were welcomed and enjoyed. It didn't turn the business into a circus, but it did make it a place that was much more fun to work in. As a result, productivity increased and so did sales. Customers enjoyed dealing with this business because the people were fun to deal with.

Have a look around your workplace. Are the people working there having fun? Do they look like they are enjoying themselves? Does anyone ever come up to you and tell you their latest joke? If not, maybe you need to encourage a lighter atmosphere.

If you work at home or by yourself, you may need to be more inventive. When I have worked like this, I always kept a few books of my favourite cartoonists handy. If I was feeling a little flat I could flick through a few pages and soon have a smile on my face, which made my day go that little bit easier.

Most workplaces are very serious. There really is no need for them to be like this, so spread a bit of cheer and lighten up. Learn to laugh, or keep laughing, no matter how bad things get.

84 Learn to handle stress

Stress can be a killer. It is without a doubt one of the conditions that small business operators are particularly prone to. Stress affects us all in different ways and we should not underestimate the effect it can have on us, both physically and mentally.

Stress is like putting on weight. You don't just get up one morning and find that you have gained 20 kilograms. Gradually, over a few years, your weight increases and all of a sudden you weigh 20 kilograms more than on the day you were married. In the same way, the more stress that you allow to build up, the more damage it can do.

Stress can affect you physically by causing things like ulcers, disturbed sleep, lethargy, headaches, heart problems, eating disorders, substance abuse and hair loss, to mention just a few of the more common signs. Mentally, stress can lead to anxiety and panic attacks, the development of new phobias, emotional instability and mood swings. Your doctor can provide you with information about the signs and symptoms of stress.

The hardest part of dealing with stress is figuring out what you can do to relieve it. Everyone is different. I find that when I'm suffering from stress, I need to spend a day outdoors, either fishing or going for a walk in the rainforest or spending the day at the beach. After doing this for a day, or even for a few hours, I can feel the stress leaving my body. Everyone has their own way of relieving stress; you need to identify what works for you.

If you are concerned that your stress levels are really high and you are starting to feel out of control, don't be embarrassed; simply visit your doctor and tell them exactly how you are feeling. If you don't do something about it, things will only get worse and the stress will manifest itself in increasingly startling ways the longer you ignore it.

85 **Listen to your instincts—they are normally right**

I believe that this is the most important booster tip in this book. We all have a sixth sense that tells us when something isn't right. We may find ourselves saying 'yes' to someone, while in the back of our mind there is a little voice trying to tell us that something is wrong. I have had this sensation when employing staff, when I have made major business decisions, when I have purchased particular products, and in many other situations. I have often gone ahead even though this little voice has tried to tell me otherwise. Usually these decisions have proven to be very bad ones and have ended up causing me a lot of grief or costing me a lot of money.

Likewise, there have been many times when I have met with a particular client or prospective staff member and my instincts have encouraged me to work with that person. The same applies to making a decision—if my instincts say that this is good, I will go with it.

Of course, I have no scientific evidence to prove how or why this works, but I know that it works for me. Using my instincts is now an important part of my business strategy.

While researching this book I asked a lot of business people what they felt had made them successful. Without exception, they said that there was something that they couldn't explain that either encouraged them towards a particular course of action or steered them away.

The hardest part of understanding and listening to your instincts is that there isn't a rule book that tells you how to do it. If I find myself in a situation that I have some reservations about, I ask for some time to consider the proposition. This allows me to mull over the possibilities and gives my instincts a chance to get through to me.

At times our decisions become clouded. If we are short of money and someone comes along offering a great deal that would relieve financial pressure in the short term, we are tempted to go for it even if our instincts are ringing alarm bells—for instance, the guy offering the money is carrying a violin case and likes to be called 'Crusher'.

My advice, and the advice of the people I have asked for their booster tips, is to learn to listen to your instincts. If you don't have a clear feeling of 'yes' or 'no' about a decision, then take some time to think about it. Talk about the pros and cons with someone you trust who you know will be completely honest and tell you what they really think and not what you want to hear.

86 Take regular holidays, even though there is never a good time

I am always telling people to go on holidays; in fact, I believe it's the best marketing advice I can offer. Many of the people I see come in looking worn-out, tired, jaded and generally ready to pack it in. My job is to tell them that they will need to put a pile of energy into building their business back up, and I can see in their faces that they have nothing left to give. They are completely shattered.

What chance do they have of building their business back up from this stage? The obvious answer is: not much. Successful businesses are as much about energy and enthusiasm as they are about anything else. I believe that a combination of the two, with a little cash thrown on top, can help you do just about anything.

You need to be fresh and sharp to succeed. In the same way that I have recommended taking time out on a regular basis and keeping up with your hobbies, you need to take regular holidays. I'm not talking about taking the afternoon off to catch up on paperwork; I'm talking about getting completely away from anything that causes you stress. If your business will fall apart because you aren't there for a few weeks, then you really have more serious problems to look at.

There is never a good time to have a holiday, there is never enough money in the bank, there are literally thousands of reasons not to go and there always will be. The problem is that if you don't have a good break on a regular basis, you will slowly but surely lose your edge and burn yourself out. No matter how much you love your work, or how important you feel you are, if you don't have regular holidays you won't get a medal from the small business martyr association—all you'll get is more stress and less success.

Try to plan your holidays on a semi-regular basis so that you always have something to look forward to. A good friend of mine who has a very stressful job takes one week's holiday every three months or so. His philosophy is that he only ever has a couple of months to work without a break, so he is always looking forward to his next holiday. He doesn't always go to exotic locations; often it's just a week off to do some gardening and catch up on things around the house and perhaps play a few rounds of golf. I like his philosophy and I believe that it's a good way to survive stressful situations in the long term.

I therefore recommend that you take holidays as often as you can and do the things that you really enjoy and that will help you to unwind.

87 Develop your negotiating skills

Life is all about negotiating. We see young children developing this skill when it comes to eating their greens. We negotiate with them: 'Eat your broccoli and you can have some dessert.' The decision is then up to them. How badly do they want the dessert? 'If I eat half of my broccoli, can I have half of my dessert?' The negotiations go back and forth. In some instances, it's non-negotiable; in others, there is room for flexibility—normally depending on the energy level of the parent.

Good negotiating skills are an asset that can be used all day every day. Now, I would like to make the point that there is a difference between negotiating and being tough in business. The ideal outcome of a negotiation is that both parties walk away feeling some degree of satisfaction. To negotiate you need to be flexible and willing to listen to the other person's point of view.

The most successful people I know are excellent negotiators. I have often spoken to them about this skill, assuming that it was a natural ability. That's far from the case. Many of these people realised that winning in every situation requires someone to be the loser. In this way, bridges get burned, people become less willing to work with you again, and so on. These smart people have realised that they can get what they want by being flexible and making their opponent feel like a winner as well.

The keys to negotiating success are:

- Have a clear bottom line or outcome in your head. You won't go below this.
- Look at the situation from the other person's point of view.
- Be patient and never lose your cool.
- Ask the other person if they are happy with the outcome at the end of the negotiation.
- Be prepared to walk away.

There are many different courses available on negotiating. I strongly recommend that you find the time to do one. You will be amazed at how many areas of your life can benefit from good negotiating skills. If you haven't got time to do a course, watch two children discussing a toy swap and you'll see all the necessary skills being played out in front of you.

88 Be supportive of the community where you make your living

I am a strong believer in being a good corporate citizen. This simply means that you put something back into your community. There are many ways that you can be a good corporate citizen and I have listed a few of them below:

- Support a local charity (such as the children's ward at the local hospital).
- Sponsor a children's sporting team.
- Give your time freely to a good cause—make soup or deliver care packages to the needy every once in a while.
- Offer to talk to children at your local school on their next careers day.
- Give old office equipment to a needy cause—old computers have little resale value, and the local school or day-care centre may be able to use them.
- Give your expertise to charity—we offer marketing advice freely to several local charities.

If you make your living out of the community, you should be prepared to put something back in. If you haven't got a lot of money, how about giving a little of your time? I strongly believe that if you are a good corporate citizen, your community will be good to you.

89 Use photographs to record your progress

When you are in the midst of running your own business, time seems to fly. Often it's hard to know if you are moving forward or just treading water. A good friend of mine told me many years ago how he uses photographs to gauge if his business is moving ahead. I have used his advice ever since. I take a lot of photographs of my premises, my staff, any promotions or events that we hold, and any other general bits and pieces that have some relevance to me. Along with these photographs, I also collect pieces of promotional material, samples of office stationery, letters from customers, and so on, which I keep in a photo album. They provide a snapshot of my business during its various stages of evolution.

The album is a time capsule of sorts which shows that we are moving forward. I look at the album from my first business almost 20 years ago and, apart from realising how young (and thin) I looked, I see that I have come a long way. This adds a perspective that is sometimes hard to get in any other way.

Keep a pictorial history of your business. If you find that it looks the same today as it did ten years ago, you might need to move things along a bit. It's also a great tool to show people who may be looking to buy your business, as it adds flesh to the profit and loss statement.

90 Know when to call it a day

It's important to know when to get out of the business you are in. If you are at the end of your tether emotionally, financially and physically, it may be time to call it a day. Unless there is something potentially life changing on the horizon, today may be the day when you need to say, 'That's it—I'm going to sell my business, or close it down, or go bankrupt.' This is a decision that shouldn't be taken lightly, but it shouldn't be the hardest decision you've ever taken in your life.

We all get very attached to and emotional about our businesses, but believe me when I say that there is life after they are gone. I have some very close friends whose large companies went broke, and they all say that the day they closed was a huge relief. They could now get on with their lives, and they did.

Your situation may be at the other end of the scale: business is good and getting better, you have plenty of assets built up, and now you are thinking about selling out and pursuing another interest, or perhaps just taking a well-deserved extended holiday. Whatever the case, it's important to know when enough is enough and it's time to move on. Don't be one of those people who, for whatever reason, just can't seem to let go. You own the business, so you make the decisions.

Success in business often comes down to timing. I often hear the comment, 'I stayed in for too long and lost the lot. If I'd got out early, I'd have made a killing.' Do *you* know when to call it a day?

91 Break the habit of doing things the way they've always been done

Businesses evolve over time. Often the way things are done is based simply on habit—on the fact that this is the way they have always been done. Habits can be good or bad. I urge you to look honestly at the way your business operates at every level to see if there are ways that you could improve what you are doing.

Very few businesses wouldn't benefit from this kind of appraisal. Something as simple as putting timers on all your electrical switches could save you hundreds, if not thousands, of dollars a year. Are there other business opportunities that have evolved as a result of your business's own natural evolution? If you run a truck around town all day, perhaps you could sell advertising space on the vehicle to another company; or maybe you could join forces with a few other businesses to increase your buying power for fuel. There are hundreds of ways to break old habits and, in the process, save money and work more efficiently. The irony is that it takes time and money to find these new methods. In the long run, though, you will win out.

In recent years I have read a lot of books by Dr Edward de Bono, the man credited with developing the concept of lateral thinking. I strongly recommend that you read some of his books to help you think about your business and the steps that you take in making business decisions. Fresh eyes can lead to fresh ideas.

The way you work is another area that is often dictated by old habits. Just because you have been disorganised for 20 years doesn't make it OK. Changing old business and personal habits takes time, energy and a real commitment from you, but at the end of the day you are the one who will benefit the most from improving the way you work. I got into the habit of working six days a week, whether I needed to or not. I would waste time during the week because I knew that I could finish off my work on Saturday, but my home life suffered as a result. It took me a while, but I changed my old habits and decided that I would complete all of my work between Monday and Friday and spend the weekends doing the things that I really enjoy. It has changed my life.

92 Don't be afraid to make changes (name, location, etc.)

We are living in an age characterised by a faster rate of change than ever before, and there is no reason to believe that this rate of change will slow down. Resistance to change, and stress associated with change, are real issues and there are now many companies that help businesses and individuals to deal with change. To thrive in this modern business world, we all need to be open to—indeed, embrace—change.

Many companies are concerned about making changes of any sort. Something as simple as painting the outside of the building becomes a long-term project involving a cast of thousands. I don't know if it's because of the industry I am in, but I find that change is normally a good thing. Advertising agencies change their name once a week—in fact, it's a standard joke that people in our game write their own business cards in pencil.

I have never once changed my business's name or location and suffered as a result. I have recommended to many clients that they change their business name, for one reason or another; some have done so and have done very well. Many old-time business people, however, feel that their customers won't understand a change of name or image. Customers aren't stupid, so I don't see what the problem is. To me it's a healthy sign to see a company change its name and image on a semi-regular basis. How often depends on your business, but I believe that corporate images should last a minimum of five years and a maximum of ten. If your business name no longer reflects what your company does, change the name. If it is handled well by you and your staff, you will generally have an increase in business as a result of the free publicity associated with the name change.

Some people may worry that their customers will think that they are in financial trouble if they change their name or premises. If you develop a new corporate image, perhaps move to a new office, introduce new uniforms, and so on, customers are likely to perceive that your business is prospering, rather than in trouble.

I always recommend that you seek good advice when undertaking a corporate rebranding. A fresh set of eyes can offer some excellent ideas and recommendations.

There are many other areas of both business and personal life that can be changed. Embrace change and all that it encompasses and you will find that your confidence in many areas of your life will increase. Changes can act as real motivators; they can reignite passion and enthusiasm that can start to lag, over time, in any business.

93 Keep copies of important documents

Over the years we all accumulate an amazing array of paper-work. Boxes and boxes of the stuff seem to fill every corner and cupboard. By law you are required to keep many documents relating to income and expenditure for taxation purposes; however, a lot can be thrown away or, even better, recycled.

Deciding what should be kept and what should be ditched is difficult. If you are like me, you will keep every scrap of paper you have ever produced and sooner or later you will run out of space. If you are at the other extreme, you will have nothing—the true paper-less office. Deciding on a happy medium is prob-ably the best advice. However, you should always keep the originals, along with copies, of important documents.

In the course of my business I have been involved in several legal cases where I have sued companies, either for not paying their bills, or for selling me faulty products, and even in one case for copyright infringement. These cases sometimes went on for years, and often old documents that I had saved ended up playing a major role in my winning the case. For example, one case required a diary of mine from six years before to be produced as evidence that a certain meeting took place.

I now save all of my diaries for at least ten years. Business registration certificates, contracts, letters of commendation, important reports, tax returns and insurance policies are all important documents that can get lost in the pile of paper-work. I now have a file that I call 'Important Documents'. I make copies of any document that I feel is important and I store it in this file, which I keep outside of the office. This way, I know that if the office were to burn down at least I have copies of documents that I need and that I would find hard to replace.

The same principle applies to backing up computer data. Whenever you back up your files (and if you don't, you should), make two copies—one for home and one for the office. After all, if your office burns to the ground your insurance will give you new computers, but you won't have any data to put in them.

For really important documents, such as wills, I keep a copy in the office, a copy at home and a copy with my lawyer.

The only time this booster tip is important is when you really need it. A number of my associates who have lost their business premises as a result of a natural disaster have said that the disruption to their operations would have been reduced considerably if they had stored copies of data and important documents elsewhere.

Notes

....
....
....
....
....
....
....
....
....
....
....
....
....
....
....

Booster Tips Action List

Things to do   **Completed**

1. ....
2. ....
3. ....
4. ....
5. ....
6. ....
7. ....
8. ....
9. ....
10. ....

12 | Planning for the future booster tips

We constantly hear and read about the importance of setting goals and making plans for the future. I am a firm believer in setting goals on both a personal and a business level. It's important to know where you are going and whether or not you are getting there. It's equally important to understand—and plan for—the external factors that can affect your goals, and your business in general. This section addresses planning for your business and yourself, now and in the future.

The ideas we'll talk about in this section are:

#94 Know exactly where you are going
#95 Know exactly how you are going to get there
#96 Stay aware of, and up-to-date with, what is happening in your industry
#97 Competition—you need to be better than the rest
#98 Always have a plan for when things go wrong
#99 Be aware of your business's peaks and troughs
#100 Don't just look at your business in terms of facts and figures
#101 Set your business up so that someone will want to buy it

94 Know exactly where you are going

Running a business of any size can be truly challenging. Apart from doing your day-to-day work, there are many other issues that you have to think about. These issues can be anything from juggling finances, to worrying about an unhappy customer, to feeling guilty because you aren't spending enough time with your family.

I often meet people who have become totally absorbed by their business, and I have to admit that there have been many times when I have been guilty of the same obsession. At these times, it's easy to lose track of what you are working towards.

This booster tip encourages you to have a clear picture in your mind of where you want to be in 12 months, two years, three years, and so on. Some businesses just seem to be running on autopilot: everything just happens of its own accord, and there is no real enthusiasm being injected into the business.

By knowing what you are working towards, you constantly have goals. These goals may be financial, personal, spiritual, or a combination of all three. There is a very good reason why you should take the time to write down your goals: because it works.

All of the truly successful business people that I have met share one common characteristic: they are working towards certain goals. Their goals may change many times in their life, or in the life of their current business, but without exception they are driven forward by the desire to achieve these goals.

I have both small goals and large goals. I know where I want to be financially at the end of each year, and I know what type of work I want to be doing. I also know where I want to be in five years time. This helps me to get through those tough times when I'm tempted to ask myself whether it's worth it.

For some reason, the goals themselves aren't as important as just having them. I believe that they give you the drive that is necessary to succeed in business.

95 Know exactly how you are going to get there

Take the time to write down a plan. It can be as complex or as simple as you feel is necessary. It's a plan for you to follow and to give you direction. My yearly plan falls into three categories:

Personal
My personal plan outlines what I want to achieve in the coming year on a personal level. Basically, I cover the areas of my life that I would like to focus more attention on. Some years it has been to work smarter, to spend more time with my family, to go fishing more often, to be a better communicator, or to learn to play the guitar. I use this plan to draw my attention to the areas of my personal life that I feel need some work. I also include things like holidays or special trips in my personal plan so that I can look forward to them.

Financial
My financial plan outlines what I want my business to achieve in the coming year in financial terms. It's basically an overview of how much business I expect to attract and how much I expect my costs to be, and the overall end result.

Business
This plan covers what direction I would like to take the business in during the coming year. What type of customers do I want to attract? What type of work do I want to do? Are there any special purchases, such as a new vehicle or new equipment, that I want to make in the coming year?

All of the above takes about three pages and an hour to write. Yet this simple task produces a document that I refer to constantly. What I especially like to do is pull out last year's plan when I sit down to write this year's plan. It's very rewarding to see those areas where I have achieved the goals listed in my plan, and it's challenging to identify the areas that still need some work.

I am a firm believer that every business should also have a good overall business plan and a marketing plan (see Booster tip #52). However, the reality is that very few do. Taking the time to prepare a simple plan along the lines that I have outlined above can really help to boost your business.

96 Stay aware of, and up-to-date with, what is happening in your industry

Knowing what is happening in your industry is more important today than ever before. Technology is changing rapidly, consumers' habits are changing just as fast and, as a result, the way we do business needs to be able to adapt quickly. Staying aware and up-to-date is essential to the survival of any modern business. The big question is: how?

We now have access to more information than at any time in history. The Internet is a great source of current and detailed information. Make yourself comfortable using the Internet and you'll be surprised at what you can find out.

Joining industry organisations is another way to stay informed. There wouldn't be too many industry groups that don't have an association of some sort that can normally be joined for a minimal cost. In return, you will have access to information and figures that would normally be difficult for you to source.

Industry publications are another excellent source of keeping up-to-date. I subscribe to a number of specialist marketing magazines, and the information contained in them is worth thousands of dollars to me. For $4.95 per issue, I have access to survey results, the latest technology information, and industry and consumer trends—all areas that are critical to a successful marketing firm.

Attending trade expos or shows is another way to keep up-to-date (and stimulated) by what is happening in your chosen field. A trade expo where there are hundreds, if not thousands, of your industry peers provides fertile ground for the exchange of information. When I was in the diving business, the main trade show worldwide was held in America every year. I attended this show several times and always left feeling that I had really gotten value for my money.

Training seminars, conferences, and even industry networking functions, are also great ways to stay up-to-date in your particular industry. If you can, join a local group; if there isn't one, why not get one going?

To boost your business, you need to stay up-to-date and current any way you can.

97 Competition—you need to be better than the rest

Competition is the lifeblood of business. In some shape or form, we all compete with many other companies. The advent of fast planes, fast Internet communication and fast couriers means that geographical distance is no longer an overwhelming constraint.

My main booster tip here is that you need to be better than the rest. Can you honestly look at your business and say that you are the best at what you do? If you can, great; but just in case, you might want to check with your customers to make sure that the picture is as perfect as you think it is.

When I first meet with a new client, I always ask them what makes them different from their competitors. Their usual response is, 'We're the best.' I'm certain that their competitors also feel that they are the best. They can't all be the best, so someone has got it wrong.

We often do surveys using mystery shoppers. This involves our company going into a business and surveying it from the customer's point of view. While we are normally contracted by the business owner, the visit is anonymous and the staff generally aren't told (at least on the first visit) that someone is coming in. I have yet to conduct a mystery shopper survey where the business has achieved a perfect score. There is always room for improvement, and it's normally a matter of being humble enough to realise that your business can be improved.

Asking your customers their thoughts on your business is another great way to make sure that you are performing well, as well as to identify areas where you could improve. This can be done with a simple questionnaire or a quick phone call. Some people are hesitant about being honest because they don't want to offend you, so it's important that you take the pressure off them by explaining what you are trying to achieve and how you value their feedback.

From my experience, most business operators already have a feel for the areas that need improving. It's more a matter of not knowing what to do about an issue, and that gets back to asking someone else for advice or trying out a few different ideas.

The best businesses tend to thrive because they are committed to being the best.

98 Always have a plan for when things go wrong

Most airlines around the world have a public relations plan in place in the unfortunate event that one of their planes crashes. If this does happen, a button is pressed and the public relations team takes over. Normally within minutes of the accident, a press release is issued and the public relations team works on trying to minimise the damage caused to the airline's image. This can include things like covering up the signage on the wreckage so that the company's logo isn't broadcast around the world on the evening news. This is called crisis management, and any large business that has the potential for some form of crisis normally has such a plan in place.

That things sometimes go wrong is a simple fact of life. Our day-to-day problems may not be as dramatic as an airline's, but to us they are very distressing. Having a plan for when things don't work out can not only be reassuring, it can also help you to survive a business crisis that would otherwise send you broke. Having no comment to make about a problem always looks bad on television, as reporters tend to make it look like you don't care.

You may be wondering what could possibly go wrong in your business that could be classed as a crisis. I live in a tourist town with over 800 tourist-related businesses. There wouldn't be many of them that don't involve some form of risk, and occasionally people get hurt and some even die. While this is a tragedy, it's made worse by the fact that the companies themselves fall apart when something bad happens. I certainly don't mean to sound callous, but if your business involves people hand-feeding sharks, there is a chance that someone will be bitten. Prepare a plan just in case, put it where it can be found quickly in the event that a crisis happens, and make sure that everyone knows what to do.

Also have a plan in place in the event that something goes wrong in your business that affects customer satisfaction. If you can't deliver what you promised, or if the wrong part has been delivered, make sure that your business can act quickly to sort out the problem and keep the customer happy.

Regardless of the size of the problem, have a plan ready just in case you need it.

99 Be aware of your business's peaks and troughs

Most businesses have times when they are busy and times when they are quiet. For some businesses, these peaks and troughs can occur during the day—for example, restaurants are obviously busiest around meal times and quieter in-between. For other businesses, these peaks and troughs may be more widespread, perhaps extending over certain months of the year. Some businesses even have cycles of busy years followed by quiet years.

Working out your peaks and troughs takes a little time, but it's worth the effort. Most business operators already have an idea of the overall trends for their business, based on their bank account balance throughout the year. But there is a lot more information that can be collected and used to your advantage.

For example, I used to open my business in the period between Christmas and New Year. I did this for three years in a row, in the belief that I would be letting my clients down if I didn't. What happened was that the phone never rang and no work came in. Advertising and marketing their business isn't the main thing on people's minds at this time of the year. What's more, most of my clients were relaxing on the beach in some exotic location while I was sitting around waiting for the phone to ring. In the fourth year I made the decision to close the office during the break and, while I may have missed out on the odd job, I definitely started the year feeling fresh and revitalised.

A client of mine runs a restaurant that used to be open for breakfast, lunch and dinner. While the restaurant was very successful, there were definite peaks and troughs during the day. After looking at the figures very closely and monitoring the number of people who dined at specific times during the day, it soon became obvious that breakfast was a waste of time that was actually costing money. The client stopped opening for breakfast and although his turnover dipped slightly, his overall profits went up.

It may seem obvious to you and me, but there are a surprising number of businesses that just look at the amount in the cash register at the end of the day. Smart business operators monitor their income over time to determine trends.

Recently I was going on a boat cruise for the day. There were two restaurants on the marina, in a simply stunning environment. Hundreds of people were milling about by nine o'clock, waiting to board the various cruise boats. One restaurant had opened early, while the other opened only about ten minutes before everyone boarded the boats to leave. The restaurant that was open and serving breakfast was packed, and I couldn't understand why the other restaurant didn't open earlier to take advantage of this daily glut of customers. I asked the owner and he said that while there were lots of people, no one stopped to eat. I found this hard to believe, given that the other restaurant was literally bursting at the seams. How well did the second restauranteur know his potential customers?

What information can you glean from studying your business's peaks and troughs?

- You can identify when you business makes most of its income.
- You can identify when you need extra staff and when you don't.
- You can determine if it's financially viable to be open at the times you are.
- You will be able to target business to fill your quiet periods.
- You can plan any major purchases around your cash flow or busy times.
- You can plan your holidays around your quiet times.

I am a firm believer that the more you know about your business and your customers, the more successful you will be and the greater your chances of boosting your business.

100 Don't just look at your business in terms of facts and figures

Business success can be measured in many different ways. Unfortunately, a lot of people think only in terms of profit and loss, without taking into account the many other considerations that go towards making a business successful.

I often meet with clients whose businesses are struggling financially, and I feel that this affects their enthusiasm and stops them from thriving. They feel like failures because their bank account isn't full. This begins a cycle where their survival is threatened because they have adopted a defeatist attitude. The fact that they produce a great product, have excellent relationships with their staff, put a lot back into the community, and manage to balance running a business with looking after their families indicates success. However, this more balanced view of success is swamped by the feeling of failure associated with struggling to make ends meet.

I go to great pains to point out the areas where they are succeeding and that, given time, the financial results will follow. I would encourage anyone in business to write down the areas where their business is successful. This is very rewarding and it adds perspective, often when it's needed the most. If you are running your own business, you are already successful because you have taken a risk that many others would shy away from.

Ask yourself the following questions:

- Are you proud of what you do, and do you truly believe that you give 100 per cent towards being the best you can be?
- Have you established strong relationships with customers, staff, suppliers and other people that you deal with on a regular basis?
- Have you managed to balance work and home?
- Do you live a healthy lifestyle?

- Do you give praise and show sincere appreciation where it's due?
- Do you love what you do?

We all get caught up in the daily grind of profit and loss and often overlook those areas where we have so much to be proud about. Boosting your business is as much in your head as it is in your cash register.

101 Set your business up so that someone will want to buy it

The eternal hope for most business owners is that, at some stage, someone will come to them with a big bag of money and offer to buy them out. After all, this is the reward for all the hard work, stress and financial risk they have taken on.

Setting up your business so that someone will want to buy it involves looking at your business from the perspective of a prospective buyer from day one. What are prospective buyers looking for? The obvious answer is that they want to make a return on the money they plan to invest in your business. In many cases, though, there are other factors to consider as well. Sometimes people are looking to buy a lifestyle; sometimes they just want to stop working for other people and are content to make a reasonable income; sometimes they want to eliminate the competition. Whatever their motivation, you can make your business more attractive by planning ahead.

There are three main ways to increase the appeal of your business, regardless of its size, to potential buyers:

1. *Show that your business is built on solid foundations.* This can be achieved by having a business plan and a marketing plan. Even if they are only simple and straightforward, it shows that you are building your business in a strategic way, not just a haphazard way. Having customer testimonials, and even supplier testimonials, about your business is also advantageous because they show that you are good at what you do. Prepare simple graphs that show how the business has grown in the past. These graphs can include turnover, number of customers, after-tax profit, and even the volume of goods that you buy to resell. All of these graphs should show increases.

2. *Have a clean business slate.* Make sure that your tax and business records are up-to-date and accurate, and that any issues with customers or suppliers have been resolved. Ongoing

disputes can make your business less appealing. Ensure that legal documents are filed as required, and that things like leases are all in order and current.

3. *Show the potential of the business.* This is the key area that prospective buyers are looking for. Are there ways to increase the amount of business and the number of customers—in other words, is there potential for growth? This can be achieved showing industry trends, local business activity for your region, the degree of customer loyalty (do your customers keep coming back?), and continued growth in your turnover (or at least consistent profits). The prospective buyer will have their own reasons for wanting to buy your business and they will tend to have their own ideas about where the potential of the business really lies. You are simply pointing out some of the attractive features of the business that they may not have considered.

There are, of course, other factors that are important, and this is where your accountant and legal representative come into play. Some buyers won't be interested in any of the above; they will want only to see your profit and loss statements.

From my own experience, and that of successful business people I have discussed this subject with, planning ahead for the day you sell your business and building this into everything that you do will ultimately pay off at the crucial time.

Notes

....
....
....
....
....
....
....
....
....
....
....
....
....
....
....

Booster Tips Action List

Things to do   **Completed**

1. ....
2. ....
3. ....
4. ....
5. ....
6. ....
7. ....
8. ....
9. ....
10. ....

Bonus section—20 more booster tips

The bonus section has become a feature of my books. It's designed not only to add value, but also to provide a place for some of my favourite ideas spanning all of the categories covered earlier.

The ideas we'll talk about in this section are:

#102 Don't be afraid to charge what you're worth
#103 Monopolies—the ultimate competition
#104 Learn to delegate
#105 Become a spokesperson
#106 Try to win an award for your business
#107 Don't let a bad experience leave you feeling jaded
#108 Don't lose a good customer over a few cents
#109 Enjoy the journey
#110 Constantly strive to improve and boost your business
#111 Surround yourself with successful people
#112 Get to know your bank manager
#113 Make your business environmentally friendly
#114 Make your business a good place to work
#115 Learn to manage your time
#116 Don't be afraid to be unconventional
#117 Read as much as you can
#118 Persevere, persevere, persevere

#119 Be open to ideas, suggestions and recommendations
#120 Spend a few hours each week surfing the Internet
#121 Compile your own operations manual

102 Don't be afraid to charge what you're worth

Most business operators struggle with charging the right amount. If you don't charge enough you can go broke, and if you charge too much you might not get any customers. Hence, pricing your services and products correctly is critical.

A good friend of mine, who is a very successful businessman, once said to me: 'Someone has to be the most expensive, so it may as well be you. But if you're going to charge like you're the best, make sure you *are* the best.' This is a philosophy that I have adopted and it has worked well. I feel that I charge what I am worth, but I make absolutely certain that my clients get the best service possible. I deliver what I promise on time and on budget, and I guarantee the results.

No one likes to pay top dollar for a product or service only to feel that they have been ripped off. Offering good value for money is a sure way not only to keep your customers, but also to attract new customers.

A lot of businesses that undercharge don't realise they are doing so. They may underestimate the amount of time required to finish a job, or they may quote low in the belief that if they're not the cheapest they won't get the job. After a while in business you realise that there are a lot of customers out there, and that if you are good at what you do word of mouth will keep them coming to you.

It's also worth remembering that it's easy to reduce your prices, but it's hard to increase them. If you are setting up a business and trying to determine what prices you should be charging, do some research and find out how much your competitors charge. Let your customers know that your prices are introductory or special prices, and over time establish a pricing structure that works for you. Don't give your products or services away for nothing. Having lots of customers, but making no money, is the easiest way to go broke.

I was recently asked to do a marketing evaluation for a publishing company that had been around for a very long time.

The business sold a lot of products, but they never seemed to get ahead. They promoted their main product, a magazine, in the form of a subscription where the customer paid for four copies and received the fifth copy for free. For each subscriber the company was losing $10, so the more customers they attracted the worse their financial position became.

You would be surprised at how many companies are selling products and services at a loss and they don't even know it.

103 Monopolies—the ultimate competition

I have had a reasonable amount of experience working for companies that are monopolies. This basically means that they don't have any competitors. To most of us, that sounds like heaven. You can charge what you like, customer service doesn't really matter because the customers have nowhere else to go, and as long as there is a demand for the product or service, you can't possibly go wrong. Guess again.

In many ways, monopolies face the toughest competition there is—the mythical competitor. One client of mine was a taxi company. They provided a great service, the cars were excellent, the drivers were generally very good, and the waiting time for taxis averaged only three minutes. But the company was the target of numerous complaints and they couldn't understand why. On the surface their business was really well run, and so they were at a loss as to why they always seemed to get bad press in the local paper.

The main reason was that their customers had no other taxi company to compare this business to, so they compared them to the perfect mythical taxi company. This mythical taxi company would never be late, the fares would always be less than expected, the cars would always be better and the drivers would all be models of perfection.

If your business has no competition, you have to provide better products and services than do businesses with lots of competitors. Monopolies are a whole new ball game and, given the choice, I would much rather be up against concrete competition that I know I can outperform than a mythical competitor that I have no chance of beating.

104 Learn to delegate

Most small businesses have key personnel, such as the owner or manager. These people, who are supposed to be at the helm of the business, are often instead inundated by demands on their time 'below deck'. It is very hard to move forward in your business if you are bogged down in all the day-to-day activities. This is an area that I have struggled with often over the years. It's often easier to do things yourself, rather than take the time to explain to a staff member how to do a particular job and then follow up to make sure that it's done properly.

When I started to observe successful business people, I was surprised to find that while their days are full, they tend to start and finish work at a reasonable hour. They have a strong support team around them. And they don't waste time doing small or repetitive jobs that someone else could do. Instead, they expend their energy and personal resources on making decisions that will move the business forward.

For years I drove all over town dropping off documents to my clients. By the time I had got myself organised, got in the car, driven to the client's premises, stopped and had a chat, done a few other chores and then headed back to the office, I was spending about an hour for every drop-off I did. During a typical week, I would probably make up to 15 deliveries, so I was losing up to 15 hours a week just to save a few dollars in courier charges. When I realised how much of my time was being wasted in this way each week, and that instead of saving me money it was sending me broke, I quickly adopted the services of a courier.

Delegation is a hard skill to learn and one that doesn't come naturally for many people. If you are one of these, I strongly recommend that you do a course or read a book on how to delegate. Some of my clients have found it particularly helpful to ask their friends and associates who are good at delegating for tips and advice.

105 Become a spokesperson

Spokespeople are those people the media contact when they are looking for a comment on a particular issue. For example, if you run a restaurant and the local council changes its bylaws regarding pavement dining, the local papers and television stations might look to you, as a restaurant owner, to comment on how these changes will impact on your business and the industry in general.

If you would like to become a spokesperson for your industry, simply send a photograph of yourself along with a brief biography, outlining who you are and what issues you would be available to comment on, to your local newpapers, radio stations and television networks. By setting yourself up as an 'expert' in this way, your business will receive a lot of free publicity that will add credibility to your business and thus attract more customers.

If you feel uncomfortable at the thought of doing a radio or television interview, you could write letters to the editor of your local paper. You will be surprised by how many people read the letters to the editor and, once again, it's a way to gain credibility for your business.

Boosting your business is often about overcoming your fears and getting your name out there.

106 Try to win an award for your business

Credibility is an important factor when trying to establish relationships with new customers. People need to be convinced that your business is good at what it does and that their purchase is 'safe'. I have spoken about using customer testimonials as an excellent way to build credibility, but another equally effective credibility-building tool is winning an award.

The majority of businesses never bother to enter competitions, either because it's too time-consuming to fill out the applications, or because they feel that they have no chance of winning. I strongly believe that it's worth the time and effort of entering even if you don't think you have a chance of winning. The simple process of completing the application form will give you an objective view of your business that can be invaluable. It's almost like a series of snapshots of your business, showing how it started, how it has grown, what you have achieved and what your plans are for the future. In fact, it can provide a real shot in the arm for a floundering business that is lacking direction.

If you are fortunate enough to win an award, make sure that you tell everyone about it. Write a press release, let your customers know, put a sign up in the workshop, announce the award on your Internet site and mention it on all your promotional material. You will boost not only your morale and that of your staff, but your customers' morale as well.

If you have entered a few competitions and have had no luck, don't be discouraged. Each time you prepare a submission it will become easier, and the law of averages dictates that the more times you enter the more chances you will have of winning. There is nothing more rewarding than hanging a certificate of recognition from your industry peers on your wall for all to see.

107 Don't let a bad experience leave you feeling jaded

Anyone who has been in business for any length of time will be able to recite horror stories about staff, accountants, lawyers, marketing consultants, advertising sales reps, customers and the taxation department. It's a given that if you are in business, you will have some bad experiences along the way. What is important is how you handle the bad experiences. If you become bitter and twisted, this will rub off on to your staff and your customers.

I have noticed that successful business people all have a very positive attitude. You might be thinking, 'Here we go again, another one of those "think positive and the world will be your oyster" stories.' Well, it's true. Positive people succeed positively.

From my own experiences I can attest to the powers of a positive attitude. I have had plenty of crappy things happen in my life, starting from an early age. I grew up as an orphan and lived in some bad places. I've seen some shocking things and had some pretty nasty things done to me over the years. I had the choice of playing the victim and blaming the world for what I experienced, or accepting what happened, learning from it, forgiving people and moving on. I chose the latter. Bad things still happen from time to time, but they are generally insignificant when compared to the good things that happen in my life.

The point is that to thrive in business (and in life), you can't be a victim and spend your life blaming others. Positive people attract good things into their lives. I have seen this happen far too many times ever to be convinced otherwise.

There is an interesting Buddhist notion that the people we learn the most from about ourselves and about life are those people we find the most difficult to deal with. Our friends and family tend to accept us the way we are. They are generally forgiving and understanding, and unlikely to be our harshest critics, so they aren't much of a challenge. But consider an unhappy customer who is demanding and angry, looking for blood. We have to use all of our people skills to handle the situation well; we need to be calm and very patient, when all we really want to do is to tell the person to get out. In other words, we are challenged by them.

Every time you face a difficult situation, try to learn from it. By facing up to challenges, your skills will grow and ultimately increase your chances of boosting your business.

108 Don't lose a good customer over a few cents

Losing a customer over a few cents is such a waste that it's hard to believe that it happens as often as it does. There is little point in trying to attract new customers if we can't hold on to those we already have.

I recently hired a video from my local video shop. When I arrived home it was late at night and I decided that I would curl up in front of the television and watch the movie. When I opened the case, I found that it contained the wrong video. Thoroughly disgusted, I went to bed. The next day I returned the video and asked for a refund. The young woman who served me said that I should have rung them immediately to say that the movie was the wrong one. Why I should have done this I'm not sure, but apparently it was 'store policy'. She said that they would have to charge me for the movie because I could have watched it. (So now I'm a liar as well as a difficult customer.)

I pointed out that it would have made no difference if I had rung the night before, because I certainly wasn't going to get in my car and drive back to the video store in the middle of the night to exchange the video. The shop assistant huffed and puffed some more and then asked me what I expected her to do. I said that I didn't think I should have to pay for the video. She grudgingly accepted this. Then I asked her to look up my record to see how many videos I had hired since becoming a member. With some more huffing and puffing she checked the computer and told me that I had rented over 1000 videos. (Obviously, I have too much time on my hands!) This equated to almost $6000 in video hire charges, and goodness knows how much in drinks and packets of chips. I vowed never to return to that business, and I haven't.

Instead of apologising, giving me a free video hire and generally placating an upset customer, one shop assistant has cost that business a good customer. Where is the logic in this? I don't even blame the girl that served me—I blame the business manager for having such regimented and clearly ridiculous rules.

Don't lose sight of the long-term value of your customers. If there is a showdown over a few lousy dollars, be prepared to compromise.

109 Enjoy the journey

Owning, operating or managing a small business is demanding. You can be pulled in a hundred different directions at once, and the pressure can sometimes be overwhelming. It's easy to get into the routine of always thinking ahead and planning for tomorrow, which is important, but at times you need to stop and take notice of where you are at *now*.

Successful business people often comment that they find the journey far more stimulating and enjoyable than actually arriving. Some even lose interest once they have built a business up to the level where it's highly profitable and running well, because the challenge is gone.

We can all benefit from remembering to enjoy the journey. The good times are as important as the tough times, and both combine to put you where you are right at this moment. Rather than dragging your feet into work and diving straight into the pile of paperwork on your desk, take a few minutes to chat with someone you normally don't have time to talk to. Ask them about their life, about their views on the business and where it's going, and whether they are enjoying what they are doing.

Making your own business a success is one of the most exciting and rewarding challenges that a person can take on. It may take several years to achieve financial success, but as pointed out in other sections in this book, there are many other ways to measure success. Successful business people have realised that there is a lot of enjoyment to be had along the way.

110 Constantly strive to boost your business

Good business operators are instinctively committed to constantly improving and boosting their business. However, it's easy to get into a rut, where you become so busy doing what you do that you don't notice the walls falling down around you. When you finally do get a chance to stop and take a breath, you realise that the place is coming apart at the seams.

To ensure that your business is constantly evolving and improving, you may need to put some mechanisms in place that encourage feedback and suggestions from your staff and your customers. By emphasising to them that you are committed to improving the business, you will convince them to keep giving you feedback.

There are a million and one ways to improve just about any business. Knowing where to start is the hardest part. I suggest that you make the task more manageable by making a 12-month plan where, every month, you focus on one particular aspect of your business. Perhaps you will only make one significant change each month, but at least you are heading in the right direction.

111 Surround yourself with successful people

This is an oldie, but a goodie. Surround yourself with positive, successful people and some of what they have will rub off on you. For some reason, successful people are attracted to other successful people. Perhaps it's due to mutual respect. Crooks and shonks are also attracted to one another.

Wherever possible, surround yourself with motivated and positive people. If you find that you are in a group of negative people, try to distance yourself from them until they become more positive or you decide once and for all that you don't need their negative energy in your life anymore.

Success can be measured in many ways, and I certainly don't consider financial success to be the only criterion. I have met many financially successful people who are mean and nasty, and always looking for someone to make a dollar out of. The successful people I am talking about are those who manage to balance a busy work and home life with a positive outlook, or those who do what they say they are going to do.

Try to be around people who have been in business for some time and have managed to survive and prosper while maintaining their sense of humour and passion for what they do. If you don't know any people like this, join a few organisations that host networking functions or business get-togethers and start looking for people to emulate.

A friend of mine recently started a club called The Abundance Club. It consists of a group of people who share similar beliefs about the nature of success and a genuine passion for sharing positive energy and thoughts with others in the group. Why not form your own club and welcome only those people with a positive attitude and a desire to be successful at what they do?

112 Get to know your bank manager

This is a great booster tip suggested to me by some of my older clients who are used to doing business on a handshake. It goes back to the days when one's bank manager really had a major influence on one's business life. Of course, most applications for finance are now processed by computers; however, it's still as important to get to know your bank manager today as it was 50 years ago.

Bank managers are busy people, so getting to meet them for a chat can be a little difficult. I suggest that you make an appointment to talk to your bank manager about your business and your financing needs. If you can't get in to see them, write them a letter, introducing yourself and explaining a little about your business. Eventually you will meet, and you can then work on developing a relationship with them. A supportive bank manager who has followed your business as it has grown can be a strong support when times get tough and banks get even tougher. Like any relationship, go into it with an open mind and a clear goal.

113 Make your business environmentally friendly

We all have a role to play in making businesses more environmentally friendly—after all, we intend on being around for a
while and I, for one, would like the planet to be in the best
possible shape while I am on it. Here are some ways we can all
help:

- Put all lights on timers, or at least make certain that the last
  person out of the office turns everything off.
- Turn off peripheral office equipment such as photocopiers
  and printers at the end of each day.
- Put signs in the toilets encouraging staff to conserve water.
- Ensure that no pollutants run into drains.
- Ensure that all company vehicles are well-maintained.
- Recycle wherever possible—paper, printer cartridges, glass
  jars, old furniture, and so on.

There are now environmental consultants who will come to
your business and identify ways in which you can become more
environmentally friendly. They basically do an audit and make
recommendations that will have a positive impact on both the
environment and your bank balance. For instance, changing
the type of lightbulbs you use can have a huge effect on your
bottom line at the end of the year, as can encouraging better use
of water and power.

I believe that it's important to be committed to becoming
more environmentally aware and friendly, and not just paying
lip service. Printing your company stationery on recycled paper
may cost a few cents more, but think of the benefits for the
planet. Like all company philosophies, environmentally aware
practices need to be generated from the top and encouraged to
infuse through the organisation.

The amount of waste generated by most businesses is quite
amazing. A client of mine used to have to order 10,000 sheets
of paper per month because they didn't have a paper recycling

system set up. Inter-office communications is another area where paper and stationery can be wasted. All it normally takes to rectify this situation is to review work practices and put a few systems in place that make environmentally friendly work practices the norm rather than the exception.

When purchasing new office equipment, how often do you ask about the energy rating of the equipment? If you are like most people, this isn't a major consideration when making a purchase—but why not conserve energy and lower your power bills at the same time?

By doing a simple audit yourself, I'm certain that you will be able to identify many ways in which your business can become more environmentally friendly. There is a definite relationship between business survival and being a good corporate citizen. I believe that by being responsible, you will be rewarded in other ways.

114 Make your business a good place to work

There has been a lot of research done over the years high-lighting the benefits of having a good working environment. The better the workplace, the more efficient the staff and the more satisfied the customers, and so the more customers you attract. Being a good workplace means that your office or shop is always clean and tidy, your equipment is the best that you can afford, the lighting is effective, there are fresh flowers in the reception area, the air smells fresh, and so on. Even something as simple as having good coffee available makes a difference.

The most wonderful element that my staff bring to our office is a sense of fun and enjoyment. Every day is filled with laughter, and we have a fantastic rapport with our clients. We joke around, play jokes on each other and generally encourage everyone to have a good time.

Of course, not every day is a bed of roses or a night at the circus; but overall we laugh more than we cry, and anyone who works with us or visits our business always comments on how much fun it is and how great the atmosphere is. We spend a lot of time, money and energy making our office look very attrac-tive, and our pride in it shows. I also believe that we have attracted a lot of business because we have such an appealing office.

We all get a little caught up in ourselves from time to time. Having a laugh, and taking some time out just to enjoy the day, can only benefit your staff and customers. Make your business a fun place to work and everyone will benefit. If your place of work seems to be filled with long faces and bad smells, maybe today is the day to give it an overhaul.

115 Learn to manage your time

One of the biggest problems facing most small business operators is a lack of time. There are more day-to-day activities that
demand your time, and as your business grows and becomes
more successful there will be even more demands on your time.

I struggled with time management for many years, because
I found it hard to say 'no' to people. As a result, I found myself
struggling to get my work done. I struggled to pay the rent,
because I was doing a lot of work for no charge. And, worst of
all, my personal life suffered, because I had to work so hard to
meet my commitments to the people I couldn't say 'no' to in
the first place that I didn't have much time left to spend with
my loved ones. Obviously, things were very out of whack and
drastic changes were needed.

I decided that I needed to develop far better time management skills. It was no fun having to work weekends to make up
for the time I was wasting during the week. Because I worked
weekends I never had a good break, so I was always tired, my
personal relationships suffered, and my health wasn't as good as
it should be. My new time management plan meant that I
wasn't allowed to work on weekends (unless there was a very
good reason, such as a mid-week fishing trip which required
that I clear my desk beforehand).

Learning to manage your time more effectively can have a
very profound effect on your life and on your business. There
are excellent books available on time management, as well as
some great courses and training seminars. Ask your friends and
business network if they can recommend a particular book or
course.

116 Don't be afraid to be unconventional

It's easy to become dull and boring in the way that you run your business. Have you ever noticed that all doctors' surgeries and accounting practices look much the same? Why? Without a doubt there is a credibility factor—which I believe is important. Your business should look professional, but there is nothing wrong with looking the part and also adding some individual touches.

Your business needs to stand out from the crowd if it is to have any chance of surviving. Being unusual and unconventional can often bring sensational results—it's just a matter of being brave enough to give it a go.

It's a very modern world out there and customers are much more savvy than ever before. Impress them, get them talking about your business, and you will succeed.

117 Read as much as you can

We are fortunate to be living at a time when books and magazines are readily accessible, generally affordable and very information-specific. If you are having a problem with a particular aspect of your business or your life in general, the chances are that there are a number of very good books offering pertinent advice and some practical solutions.

I read a lot. Often it's hard to know what to do with all the information that books provide, but I take the view that if I can pick up one or two good ideas from a particular book, it's worth its cover price many times over. (Hopefully, you'll have found more than just a few good ideas from this book.)

The same principle applies to trade magazines and other publications that are specific to your industry. They can be a very valuable source of information. After subscribing to an industry publication for a few years, you'll find that you have compiled a great library of relevant information.

If you haven't the time to read, consider buying books on tape. This obviously works well if you spend a lot of time in the car or travelling on trains or planes. More and more publications are coming out in this format, enabling you to take advantage of the latest information without cutting into your busy schedule.

118 Persevere, persevere, persevere

There is nothing more frustrating than having people tell you that good things take time, and that patience is a virtue. Nevertheless, in business, timing does seem to have a real bearing on whether you will succeed; thus, my advice is: persevere, persevere, persevere.

Successful business people are generally tenacious, prepared to take risks and willing to persevere. They seem to have an almost instinctive understanding that if they do everything right, the business will ultimately be successful; it's just a matter of time.

Perseverance is also necessary when it comes to dealing with staff, customers and suppliers on a day-to-day basis. Not everyone thinks the way you do, and some people take longer than others to pick things up. Try to be patient and keep an eye on the 'big picture'.

I have seen a lot of business people jump from idea to idea, and from scheme to scheme, without ever really making a go of any of the businesses they start. Often they quit and move on to the next thing just as the business is about to start working. Some people even sabotage themselves out of a subconscious fear of success. They may quit their job just as they are up for a promotion, or sell their business just as it's starting to boom and their hard work is beginning to pay off. If this sounds like you, it might be time to review your strategy and perhaps go to someone for advice.

Patience, perseverance and confidence that you are doing what's right for your business will help you to survive and prosper.

119 Be open to ideas, suggestions and recommendations

The fact that you are reading this book indicates that you are open to new and innovative ideas. Being flexible is a key to surviving. I am always impressed when dealing with successful and experienced business people who are completely open to new ideas, suggestions and recommendations. At the other end of the scale, I am amazed at how closed-minded some business owners and operators are. It's a case of doing it their way or the highway, which doesn't create an environment that's conducive to encouraging creativity and inspiration, and ultimately success.

Maintaining an open mind in business can be difficult at times. It's something that many of us have to work hard at, while others seem able to be constantly open to new ideas. Smart business operators are always asking other people what they think. It's as if they are running an ongoing market research campaign aimed at collecting as much information and as many opinions as possible to check that they are on track.

Surviving in business is about being open and smart enough to listen to other people's thoughts, ideas and suggestions. Developing a working environment that encourages input from other people, including your staff, business associates and customers, will only help your business. Installing a simple suggestion box is a good start.

120 **Spend a few hours each week surfing the Internet**

Information increases your chances of survival, and there is no better place to find information than the Internet. I strongly recommend that you take time out of your busy schedule to surf the Internet each week. Spend as much time as you can realistically afford, and let the Internet take you where it will. Follow some links and click on to banner advertisements. There is so much information on the Net that the only limit is the amount of time you have available.

As a marketing consultant I search the Internet for new and innovative ideas that I can use for my clients, and there are literally thousands of them, freely available, ready and waiting for someone to come along and download them. Every industry group is represented in some way on the Internet. It's always a good idea, therefore, to do some homework on what your peers and the competition are doing.

Some of the best websites I have seen have been put together by small, innovative companies, so don't restrict your search to the larger organisations whose sites are sometimes conservative in approach and cumbersome to navigate.

If you want to find out information about any subject at all, somewhere on the Internet it will be available. Information is a powerful business resource, so spending time finding information that you can use is an absolute asset to any business. Take the time, keep away from non-productive, time-wasting sites, and let the Internet teach you how to be better equipped to boost your business.

121 Compile your own operations manual

Many smaller business operators don't feel it's necessary or appropriate to compile an operations manual. My view is that small businesses can benefit at least as much from having an operations manual as a larger company.

An operations manual simply states how your business works. It covers what to do when opening the place up in the morning, how staff should be dressed, how to deal with customer complaints, where to order various supplies and products, company policy on the private use of work facilities such as the phone, refunds policy, and just about anything else that is relevant to the day-to-day operations of the business.

Operations manuals should be updated regularly. For this reason, they are probably best kept in a folder where pages can be added and removed. The information needs to be written in very simple, plain language, preferably in list formats.

Another important part of an operations manual is the section on what to do in an emergency. What should your staff do if they unlock the business in the morning and find that it has been burgled? Or what is the procedure in the event of an accident? In times of crisis, it's very reassuring to have a step-by-step plan that anyone can use.

Operations manuals should also contain a list of contact numbers and alternatives, identifying who should be contacted and when, and what to do if a particular person can't be reached.

Another important point with operations manuals is to ensure that everyone knows where it is and that all the relevant people have read it. If a crisis arises and people are rummaging through boxes trying to find the folder, it's a waste of time.

Having an operations manual also shows that you are organised and professional, and gives staff and customers confidence in your organisation.

Increase your chances of survival by developing a simple, but functional operations manual and then make sure that everyone reads it and knows where to find it.

Notes

....
....
....
....
....
....
....
....
....
....
....
....
....
....
....

Booster Tips Action List

Things to do   **Completed**

1. ....
2. ....
3. ....
4. ....
5. ....
6. ....
7. ....
8. ....
9. ....
10. ....

Appendix:
Blank forms that may
come in handy

The following forms have been designed to illustrate a number of ideas raised in this book. Feel free to adapt them for use in your business.

Credit request form (for your customers)
Goals and objectives form
Professional services checklist
Job description form (position description)
A checklist for employing staff
A step-by-step marketing plan
Insurance checklist
A stress checklist
A de-stress checklist
Developing an Internet plan

Credit request form (for your customers)

The aim of a credit request form is to determine if you want to extend credit to another business. It's also an opportunity to explain your payment terms (when you want your accounts to be paid). Always check references and look for credit references that are substantial. The following is designed as a guide only, and I recommend checking with your accountant for any extra information that may be required.

CREDIT REQUEST FORM

Name of company ....

Actual address ....

Postal address ....

Telephone .... Facsimile ....

Contact name .... Position ....

Name of directors/owners ....

Main bank .... Branch ....

Name of accountant .... Contact details ....

References

Company name .... Telephone number ....

Person to contact .... Average monthly account ....

Office use

Details verified by .... Date ....

Comments ....

Company name .... Telephone number ....

Person to contact .... Average monthly account ....

Office use

Details verified by .... Date ....

Comments ....

Company name .... Telephone number ....

Person to contact .... Average monthly account ....

Office use

Details verified by .... Date ....

Comments ....

Payment terms

Please verify that you are aware of our payment terms. If credit is extended to your company, payment for invoices will be required in

.... days after receiving your invoice.

I agree to the above payment terms.(*Note:* Your accountant and/or solicitor can add more details or conditions to protect you in this section.)

Signature .... Name ....

Position .... Date ....

Goals and objectives form

The importance of setting goals and objectives is well documented. Remember to set not only business goals but also personal goals. This form provides a very simple way to write down your goals. Take a copy of this page and put it where you can read it every day.

Business goals	Personal goals
Date set	**Date set** ....
Short-term (1–3 months)	**Short-term (1–3 months)**
1. .... Achieved..........	1. .... Achieved..........
2. .... Achieved..........	2. .... Achieved..........
3. .... Achieved..........	3. .... Achieved..........
4. .... Achieved..........	4. .... Achieved..........
5. .... Achieved..........	5. .... Achieved..........
Mid-term (3–6 months)	**Mid-term (3–6 months)**
1. .... Achieved..........	1. .... Achieved..........
2. .... Achieved..........	2. .... Achieved..........
3. .... Achieved..........	3. .... Achieved..........
4. .... Achieved..........	4. .... Achieved..........
5. .... Achieved..........	5. .... Achieved..........

Longer-term (6–12 months)
1. .... Achieved ....
2. .... Achieved ....
3. .... Achieved ....
4. .... Achieved ....
5. .... Achieved ....

My thoughts

Longer-term (6–12 months)
1. .... Achieved ....
2. .... Achieved ....
3. .... Achieved ....
4. .... Achieved ....
5. .... Achieved ....

My thoughts

223

Professional services checklist

This form can be used when sourcing any professional advice, including legal, accounting and marketing consultants or firms. If used correctly, it will help you to avoid employing or contracting the wrong adviser. If a professional consultant won't give you a list of referees that you can contact to verify their abilities, don't use them.

Step 1. Recommendations from friends and business associates

1. .... Telephone .... Recommended by ....

2. .... Telephone .... Recommended by ....

3. .... Telephone .... Recommended by ....

4. .... Telephone .... Recommended by ....

5. .... Telephone .... Recommended by ....

Step 2. Make appointments

Step 3. Question checklist for meeting

- ☐ A. The business was professional and appeared reputable.
- ☐ B. I was given the opportunity to explain my needs fully.
- ☐ C. The service provider explained their services and company background fully.
- ☐ D. They explained what they could do for me in a simple, clear and concise manner.
- ☐ E. Their fee structure and payment terms were explained fully.
- ☐ F. They explained what makes them different from their competitors.
- ☐ G. I was supplied with references to verify their abilities and level of professionalism.
- ☐ H. I liked the person that I dealt with.

Step 4. Comparative rating of each business (give one point for each box checked above)

	A	B	C	D	E	F	G	H	TOTAL SCORE
Business #1									
Business #2									
Business #3									
Business #4									
Business #5									

Step 5. Check references

Step 6. The business that scores the highest and is backed up by references is the one to go with

Job description form (position description)

This form can be used as a guideline for developing a position description form. The main areas to be covered are what you expect the member of staff to do, how you would like them to do it, when they should have it done, and what they will get in return.

Expectations
- [ ] What the job entails (specific details)
- [ ] The amount of work to be completed
- [ ] When it needs to be completed by

Remuneration
- [ ] Wages (paid when)
- [ ] Holiday pay
- [ ] Insurances
- [ ] Paid sick leave, maternity/paternity leave, etc.
- [ ] Any other benefits

Performance reviews
- [ ] Time periods for reviews
- [ ] How the review process works

Working conditions
- [ ] Hours
- [ ] Parking
- [ ] Other facilities
- [ ] Immediate supervisor

Company policies
- [ ] Private use of company facilities (cars, telephones, etc.)
- [ ] Visitors
- [ ] Prejudice/harassment
- [ ] Notice required for holidays
- [ ] Sick leave requirements
- [ ] Theft

Problem resolution
- [ ] Who to see if you have a specific problem

I have read and fully understand the above.

Name .... Signature .... Date ....

A checklist for employing staff

This form is designed as a simple checklist to be used when employing staff. It can form the basis of an advertisement and an interview for potential staff. Not all of the categories may be applicable to the position that you are looking to fill.

1. Job description—what would the employee be expected to do (key points)?
2. Approximate age group
3. How much experience would you like the person to have?
4. Do they need any special skills, such as languages or licences?
5. Working conditions—what they will get and when (working hours, pay, special bonuses, etc.)
6. How would you like people to apply for the position? ☐ Send a résumé by mail ☐ Send a résumé by email ☐ Send a résumé by facsimile ☐ Call to make an appointment ☐ Turn up at a specific time
7. Time—closing dates for résumés, date to have the position filled by, etc.

A step-by-step marketing plan

A marketing plan doesn't have to be complicated. The important points to remember are listed below; simply follow this guide and you will have a rough draft of a good marketing plan.

Step 1. Figures Determine exactly how much money you need to break even and how much money you would like to earn. This gives you a target to work towards.
Step 2. Market research Determine where your customers are from and if they are happy with what you are offering. If you're not sure, ask them, either in person or using a simple questionnaire.
Step 3. Attracting new customers List the types of things you plan on doing to attract new customers (for example, newspaper or radio advertisements, letterbox drops, etc.)
Step 4. Strategy for keeping existing customers Decide what steps you are going to take to make sure that your existing customers are satisfied and happy to recommend your business.
Step 5. Set a budget Determine how much your marketing will cost and when you will have to pay for it. (Tie your marketing expenses into your cash flow.)
Step 6. Set a time frame to work towards Build a 12-month calendar based on monthly marketing activity.
Step 7. Assign responsibility—who will do what
Step 8. Monitor results to ensure that what you are doing is working

Insurance checklist

There are many different types of insurance available. The following checklist identifies the main areas that normally need to be covered. Policies may have different names in different parts of the world. This form can be used when talking to an insurance broker to ensure that you are fully covered.

Areas to be insured

- [ ] Fire, theft and burglary at your work premises
- [ ] Protection from other natural disasters, such as floods, earthquakes and cyclones
- [ ] Injury to employees on the job (and on the way to and from work)
- [ ] Injury to people who visit your place of business
- [ ] Injury to people who use your products
- [ ] Damage done to or caused by company vehicles
- [ ] Loss of income caused by health problems
- [ ] Death
- [ ] Professional indemnity (lawyers, accountants, diving instructors, etc.)
- [ ] Key person insurance (in the event of the death or disability of a partner)
- [ ] Damage to equipment (computers)

Other specific insurance needs for my business:

- [ ] ....
- [ ] ....
- [ ] ....
- [ ] ....

Things to remember with any insurance policy

- [ ] Fully disclose any information that is relevant to your insurance.
- [ ] Read the small print.
- [ ] Compare policies.
- [ ] Advise the insurance company of any changes to your business.
- [ ] Remember that prevention is better than cure.

A stress checklist

Stress is one of the main causes of business failure. For this reason, it's important to be able to identify some of the most common symptoms. The more boxes you tick, the more serious your problem may be. I strongly recommend that you have regular health checks and discuss any stress-related health issues with your doctor.

Signs that stress is becoming a problem

- [ ] Changed sleeping patterns
- [ ] Changed eating habits (too much or not enough)
- [ ] Sores that take a long time to heal
- [ ] Persistent colds and flu
- [ ] Constant lethargy and fatigue
- [ ] Short temper/anger
- [ ] Blurred vision
- [ ] Headaches and general aches and pains
- [ ] Constipation
- [ ] Alcohol or drug over-use
- [ ] Loss of hair
- [ ] Lack of enjoyment of life
- [ ] Memory loss or confusion
- [ ] Chest pains or shortness of breath
- [ ] Anxiety and panic attacks
- [ ] The onset of new phobias (flying, heights, animals, etc.)
- [ ] Lack of productivity

A de-stress checklist

One of the biggest problems with being stressed is that you can forget how to de-stress. To survive in business, you need to have a very clear plan for beating stress and performing at your best. The following list identifies some effective ways to beat stress.

Ways to reduce stress in your life

☐ Learn to say 'no'

☐ Take regular holidays

☐ Eat regular, wholesome meals, no matter how busy you are

☐ Make your work environment a fun place to be

☐ Read some motivational books

☐ Take the time out to do the things that you enjoy

☐ Spend time with family and friends

☐ Do some exercise that you really enjoy

☐ Plan some quiet time in your day when you don't answer telephone calls

☐ Work a reasonable number of hours each week

☐ Remember that it's only business

☐ Don't feel guilty when you relax

☐ If you need help, don't be afraid to ask

☐ Learn to delegate

☐ Be organised

☐ Don't take life too seriously

Developing an Internet plan

The Internet has so many applications, it can be challenging deciding how best to use it. By addressing each of the topics listed below, you will begin to develop a strategic Internet plan with very clear objectives and goals.

1. Use the Internet to tell potential customers about your business and why they should use you.
    HOW CAN MY BUSINESS UTILISE THIS ASPECT OF THE INTERNET?

2. Use the Internet to make actual sales using an online booking form or ordering system.
    HOW CAN MY BUSINESS UTILISE THIS ASPECT OF THE INTERNET?

3. Use the Internet to provide back-up for your customers 24 hours a day.
    HOW CAN MY BUSINESS UTILISE THIS ASPECT OF THE INTERNET?

4. Use the Internet to collect information (customer feedback).
    HOW CAN MY BUSINESS UTILISE THIS ASPECT OF THE INTERNET?

5. Use the Internet to disperse information.
    HOW CAN MY BUSINESS UTILISE THIS ASPECT OF THE INTERNET?

6. Budget to update your website regularly.
    HOW CAN MY BUSINESS UTILISE THIS ASPECT OF THE INTERNET?

7. Spend time looking at other websites in search of new ideas.
    HOW CAN MY BUSINESS UTILISE THIS ASPECT OF THE INTERNET?

Recommended reading

Boldt L, 1999 *Zen and the Art of Making a Living*, Penguin Books, Middlesex

Bruber MW, 1995 *The E Myth Revisited*, HarperCollins, New York

Carlson R, 1999 *Don't Sweat the Small Stuff at Work*, Bantam Books, New York

Carnegie D, 1981 *How to Win Friends and Influence People*, HarperCollins, New York

Carnegie D, 1992 *How to Stop Worrying and Start Living*, Random House, London

Griffiths A, 2000 *101 Ways to Market Your Business*, Allen & Unwin, Sydney

Hailey L, 2001 *Kickstart Marketing*, Allen & Unwin, Sydney

Hopkins T, 1998 *Sales Closing for Dummies*, IDG Books Worldwide, Foster City

Kaufman R, 2000 *Up your Service*, Ron Kaufman Pte Ltd, Singapore

Matthews A, 1995 *Being Happy*, Seashell Publishers, Cairns

Morgenstern J, 2000 *Time Management from the Inside Out*, Hodder Headline Group, Sydney

White S, 1997 *The Complete Idiot's Guide to Marketing Basics*, Alpha Books, New York

About the author

Andrew Griffiths is an entrepreneur with a passion for small business. From humble beginnings as an orphan growing up in Western Australia, Andrew has owned and operated a number of successful small businesses, starting with his first enterprise—a newspaper round—at age seven. Since then Andrew has sold encyclopaedias door-to-door, travelled the world as an international sales manager, worked in the Great Sandy Desert for a gold exploration company and been a commercial diver. Clearly this unusual menagerie of experiences have made him the remarkable man he is.

Inspired by his desire to see others reach their goals, Andrew has written five hugely successful books with many more on the way. His 101 series offers small business owners practical and achievable advice. The series is sold in over forty countries worldwide.

Andrew is the founding director of The Marketing Professionals, one of Australia's best and most respected marketing and business development firms. Producing innovative solutions to common business issues, The Marketing Professionals advises both large and small business.

Known for his ability to entertain, inspire and deliver key messages, Andrew is also a powerful motivational speaker who brings flamboyancy and verve to the corporate keynote-speaking circuit.

All of this occurs from his chosen home of Cairns, North Queensland, the Great Barrier Reef, Australia.

To read more about Andrew Griffiths visit:
www.andrewgriffiths.com.au
www.themarketingprofessionals.com.au
www.enhanceplus.com.au

101 WAYS TO MARKET YOUR BUSINESS

Stand out from the crowd

Here are 101 practical marketing suggestions to help you achieve dramatic improvements in your business without investing a lot of time and money.

Simple, affordable and quick these innovative tips are easy to implement and will bring you fast results. Choose and apply at least one new idea each week or use this book as a source of inspiration for new ways to market your services, your products and your business itself.

With tips designed to take just a few moments to read *101 Ways to Market Your Business* will help you find new customers, increase the loyalty of the customers you already have, create great promotional material and make your business stand out from the crowd.

INCLUDES 20 BONUS SUGGESTIONS TO HELP YOU ATTRACT NEW CUSTOMERS AND KEEP YOUR EXISTING ONES

101 WAYS TO REALLY SATISFY YOUR CUSTOMERS

Simple ways to keep your customers coming back

Here are 101 practical tips for delivering service that exceeds your customers' expectations and keeps them coming back. In a world where modern consumers are far more informed, discerning and demanding than ever before, customer service is one of the main areas where a business can outshine its competitors.

Use these simple tips to improve your customer service and you will be well on the way to success and profitability. With tips designed to take just a few moments to read, *101 Ways to Really Satisfy Your Customers* teaches you to identify what customers expect, and details simple suggestions that will enable your business to exceed these expectations and reap the rewards.

INCLUDES 20 BONUS TIPS THAT WILL REALLY IMPRESS YOUR CUSTOMERS

101 WAYS TO ADVERTISE YOUR BUSINESS

Read this before you spend another cent on advertising

Here are 101 proven tips to increase the effectiveness of your advertising. Use these tips to understand what makes one ad work while another fails and you will save a small fortune in wasted advertising.

With tips designed to take just a few moments to read, *101 Ways to Advertise Your Business* offers step-by-step advice on how to make an advertisement, how to buy advertising space and how to make sure that your advertisement is working to its full potential. Follow the tips and your business will soon be reaping the benefits.

INCLUDES A SPECIAL BONUS SECTION CONTAINING HUNDREDS OF THE BEST ADVERTISING WORDS AND PHRASES